The New Kayak Shop

CHRIS KULCZYCKI

The New Kayak Shop

More Elegant Wooden Kayaks
Anyone Can Build

RAGGED MOUNTAIN PRESS/McGRAW-HILL
Camden, Maine ● New York ● San Francisco ● Washington, D.C. ● Auckland
Bogotá ● Caracas ● Lisbon ● London ● Madrid ● Mexico City ● Milan
Montreal ● New Delhi ● San Juan ● Singapore ● Sydney ● Tokyo ● Toronto

Ragged Mountain Press
A Division of The McGraw-Hill Companies

10 9 8 7 6 5 4
Copyright © 2001 Chris Kulczycki
All rights reserved. The publisher takes no responsibility
for the use of any of the materials or methods
described in this book, nor for the products thereof.
The name "Ragged Mountain Press" and the Ragged
Mountain Press logo are trademarks of The McGraw-
Hill Companies. Printed in the United States of
America.

Library of Congress Cataloging-in-Publication Data
Kulczycki, Chris, 1958–
    The new kayak shop: more elegant wooden kayaks
    anyone can build / Chris Kulczycki.
        p.   cm.
    Includes bibliographical references and index.
    ISBN 0-07-135786-6
        1. Kayaks—Design and construction—
    Amateurs' manuals. I. Title.

VM353.K8527 2000
623.8'29—dc21   00-055270

Questions regarding the content of this book
    should be addressed to
Ragged Mountain Press
P.O. Box 220
Camden, ME 04843
www.raggedmountainpress.com

Questions regarding the ordering of this book
    should be addressed to
The McGraw-Hill Companies
Customer Service Department
P.O. Box 547
Blacklick, OH 43004
Retail customers: 1-800-262-4729
Bookstores: 1-800-722-4726

This book is printed on 70# Citation by Quebecor
    Printing Co., Fairfield, PA
Design and page layout by Shannon Thomas
Production management by Janet Robbins
Edited by Jonathan Eaton, Alex Barnett,
    and Joanne Allen
All illustrations by John C. Harris
All photos courtesy the author and Chesapeake Light
    Craft.

Brightside, Dacron, Ensolite, Epifanes, Ethafoam,
Fastex, Interlux, Kevlar, Kunz, LapStitch, Lufkin,
Marples, MAS, Microlight, Minicel, Monel, Nikon,
Nomex, Popsicle, Porter Cable, Sandvik, Shelman,
Starrett Tools, 3M, Vise-Grips, West System, and
Z-Spar are registered trademarks.

for Annette

Contents

ACKNOWLEDGMENTS

I cannot imagine a book that's the work of only the author. Many people helped make *The New Kayak Shop* possible. My wife, Annette, is foremost among them. When I began designing and building kayaks, she put up with sawdust and wood shavings in our rugs, wet paddle jackets in our kitchen, reams of plans in our living room, and drafting projects on the dining table. When we started Chesapeake Light Craft Inc. a few years later, Annette served as the chief financial officer, helping the company grow twentyfold in eight years. In her spare time, she produced the company catalog and newsletters and proofread both editions of this book and about one hundred of my magazine articles.

John Harris, who was Chesapeake Light Craft's general manager during the eight years I owned the company, also deserves special mention. An immensely talented boatbuilder and designer, John contributed a great deal to the designs in this book. Today he is part owner and chief designer at Chesapeake Light Craft.

Though the entire staff of Chesapeake Light Craft contributed to the boats, Ed Wigglesworth, Andrew Wood, Jim Richards, Todd Starkey, and Chaim Russ deserve special mention for their work in the prototype shop. I am also indebted to the many amateur and professional boatbuilders who bought my plans, built my designs, and offered their insights and ideas.

Some parts of *The New Kayak Shop* are adapted from articles I wrote for *Sea Kayaker*, *Fine Woodworking*, and *WoodenBoat* magazines and from manuals written for Chesapeake Light Craft's kits and plans.

*The double-paddle canoe gives the most fun
for the money of any type of boat
a person can possess.*

—L. FRANCIS HERRESHOFF, *SENSIBLE CRUISING DESIGNS*

The New Kayak Shop reflects much of what I have learned in the eight years since the publication of the first edition, *The Kayak Shop.* In those years I've designed dozens more boats, taught numerous boatbuilding courses, and answered thousands of technical questions from amateur boatbuilders. My kayak designs and methods of building have been retested and refined. In teaching four courses each year at the renowned WoodenBoat School in Brooklin, Maine, I've had the opportunity to watch and assist over a hundred novices construct fine wooden kayaks. I've learned where they have difficulty and what questions and answers are common. These experiences convinced me of the need for a new, updated *Kayak Shop* that will help anyone create a fine kayak. And I do hope that after reading this book you decide to build your own boat, and that doing so gives you as much satisfaction as

it has to those thousands of other amateur boatbuilders—including me. Launching a boat you've built is truly one of life's great pleasures.

I first paddled a kayak when I was ten years old. My family spent a vacation paddling old wooden doubles on the lakes of western Poland. Those weeks launched my love of boats, particularly of kayaks. Not long after that, I built my first boat: a boxlike 6-foot pram nailed together from paneling and 2 by 4s that I'd found in our garage. My parents returned home one day to find the patio transformed into a boatyard. Not appreciative of my breakthroughs in naval architecture, they forbade me to launch my first design. But convinced that my craft was as seaworthy as RMS *Queen Mary*, I recruited a friend to help me carry it to a nearby stream for sea trials. We didn't have any oars or paddles, but that didn't matter much since our stream was only 20 feet wide and, fortunately, flowed slowly. In any case, my pram leaked too much to go far.

Though my sporting interests soon turned to rock climbing and later, sailing, my memories of kayaks and home-built boats never faded. But not until twenty years after paddling that first kayak did I decide to build my own. I'd built a few dinghies in those twenty years, and I'd even worked as a marine carpenter for a summer, so I had confidence that my kayak would come out nicely. Still, I was surprised at how well that first kayak came out. It wasn't that I was a master boatbuilder—I'll never be accused of that—but rather that plywood kayaks are easy to build. In fact, you can probably build as nice a kayak as you can buy.

Building boats has long been known to be of therapeutic value, perhaps of only slightly less therapeutic value than using them. I came upon this bit of truth while working in a rather stressful managerial position. I would return home after work tired, anxious, tense, and hating the world, but after a few hours in my shop I would emerge refreshed and relaxed. It took a year of doing this to convince me that there was a better way to spend my days; some of us are slow learners.

My endeavors in kayak design and building led me to write the first edition of this book, *The Kayak Shop*, and to start a small company to sell plans and kits for my designs. Since the book's publication some eight years ago, interest in building wooden kayaks has exploded. I estimate that the number of kayaks built by amateur boatbuilders in 1999 was twenty times the number built in 1992. Many popular magazines and newspapers have published articles about the home-built kayak phenomenon. Chesapeake Light Craft Inc., the company I started in my basement, has grown to be the largest boat-kit manufacturer in the world. Each year it ships thousands of precut kits for kayaks, pulling boats, skiffs, and sailboats, as well as thousands of sets of plans, tens of thousands of gallons of epoxy, and truckloads of plywood and fiberglass. I like to think that this is at least partially due to *The Kayak Shop*. It may interest you to know that I recently sold Chesapeake Light Craft; I'll finally have ample time to enjoy some of the boats I've designed.

The New
Kayak Shop

CHAPTER ONE

The Wooden Kayak

This book guides you through building a 15-foot, 9-inch touring kayak, an 18-foot fast sea kayak, and a 14-foot compounded-plywood flatwater kayak. Plans for these boats are reproduced and discussed in chapter 5. The methods used to build these kayaks can be applied to building boats drawn by other designers or by you.

I'll assume that you have only an elementary knowledge of woodworking; those of you who are expert boatbuilders or cabinetmakers will have to bear with us. I'll also assume that you know a little about kayaks—that is, that you've paddled a few.

The themes here are simplicity, light weight, economy, and aesthetics. The kayaks discussed here do not require that you construct large jigs and strongbacks, nor do they rely on extensive framework. You won't need to buy any unusual tools, and the materials you will use, while not available everywhere, can certainly be ordered and shipped anywhere. These kayaks are at least a third lighter than most plastic or fiberglass kayaks, yet they are rigid and strong. They can be built for a quarter of the cost of a comparable fiberglass kayak, but they often perform better. And they are, at least to my eye, quite handsome.

The boatbuilding method described here is *stitch-and-glue* construction. We'll cut the parts for the hull to shapes shown on plans generated by computer design

ABOVE: *All these boats were built using the techniques described in this book.* RIGHT: *Modern wooden kayaks are often lighter than similar fiberglass and plastic boats. This 19-foot, ½-inch Patuxent racing kayak weighs only 34 pounds. This is how I carry it to the beach.*

programs or by careful drafting and then join them temporarily with twists of copper wire or electrical wire ties. When all the parts are assembled, the hull will take its final shape. Then we'll permanently glue the hull together with epoxy and fiberglass. OK, it's a little more complicated than that, but you'll soon see that building a beautiful kayak is possible even if you flunked high-school woodshop.

Why Wood?

A tree bends and flexes thousands of times each windy day, millions of times in a year, yet it still returns to its original shape. Its branches are strong and light, yet stiff enough to hold their load of leaves. Protected by its coating of bark, a tree must resist the assaults of sun, water, and wind. Wood's light weight, strength, resistance to fatigue, and durability are what make it an excellent material for constructing your kayak.

Though wood has lower initial strength than some other materials used in boatbuilding, its other properties make up for this. Even given the availability of such exotic materials as carbon fiber, Nomex, and Kevlar, some of today's fastest multihull sailboats are built of wood and epoxy. Few craft experience the loads and the stresses faced by an ocean racing multihull and pay so high a performance price for extra weight.

Beyond weight and strength, stiffness and resistance to fatigue must be considered when selecting the material for a kayak. Studies have shown wood to be up to ten times stiffer than fiberglass by weight

The sturdy and able Chesapeake kayaks are probably the most popular home-built sea kayaks today.

and nearly six times stiffer than a composite of Kevlar and epoxy. Though these studies aren't directly applicable to kayak construction, they do illustrate that wood is a very stiff material, and a stiff boat tends to be faster, particularly in calm water, since energy is not wasted in flexing the hull.

A kayak must have more than just initial strength; it must retain its strength despite repeated cycles of tension and compression from rough seas and spirited paddling. Wood loses very little strength even after millions of cycles of loading and unloading. A tree, flexing millions of times a year, may live for hundreds or even thousands of years if man or natural disaster do not intervene. This resistance to fatigue gives wood an advantage over many materials when a long-lasting, reliable hull is the objective.

Toughness and resistance to tearing, puncturing, and abrasion are important considerations, particularly if your kayak will be launched from and landed on rocky shores. Fiberglass and polyethylene have some advantage over wood in this respect, but the toughness of a wooden hull can be greatly improved by sheathing it with a thin layer of fiberglass cloth.

Wood's traditional drawbacks have largely been solved by modern technology. The problem of rot has been greatly reduced, though not totally eliminated, by modern methods of epoxy saturation. The problem of finding suitable wood has been solved by the advent of truly high-quality mahogany plywood. And the problem of waterproof glue has been eliminated by modern epoxy systems. Current methods of building wooden boats bear little resemblance to methods used fifty years ago. Wood has become a high-tech material.

However much we appreciate the engineering properties of wood, it is wood's aesthetic qualities that are most remarkable. No other material inspires such a bond between the paddler and his craft. People seem drawn to wooden boats, perhaps as a reaction to the profusion of man-made materials that surround us. Wooden kayaks seem to feel better and paddle better than fiberglass boats. I don't know why this is; perhaps I only imagine it—but a lot of other folks imagine it, too. Many sailors have written that their wooden boats seem to be alive, a feeling they miss when they sail fiberglass boats. Well, I wouldn't go that far, but I'll admit that wooden kayaks are somehow more satisfying to paddle. Perhaps this impression can be compared to

The West River 180 is a fast touring kayak. It has a multi-chine hull and a cambered deck.

that of the fly fisherman who insists on using a split Tonkin bamboo rod even though perfectly good graphite rods are available at a quarter of the cost.

So why aren't more kayaks built of wood? Well, more and more are. I recently mentioned to the owner of one the largest manufacturers of plastic kayaks how many kits for wooden kayaks Chesapeake Light Craft had sold and his jaw dropped in amazement; wooden kayaks have become serious competitors to fiberglass and plastic boats. There has been a tremendous revival of wooden boat building in general, and kayak building in particular. But wood isn't as well suited to production building as are plastics, so mainstream builders aren't likely to use it. Still, many skilled wooden boat builders build kayaks for a small clientele.

Fortunately, wood is readily available and relatively inexpensive, and it can be worked with a minimum of tools and skills. And wood is a satisfying material to work with; its texture, appearance, and even its smell are pleasing. Most amateur builders regard forty to eighty hours of cutting, sanding, planing, and varnishing a thoroughly agreeable way to spend some free time. The labor-intensive process the production builder wants to avoid is recreation to the amateur.

Building with Plywood

When plywood kayaks are mentioned, some older paddlers may recoil, thinking of slab-sided monstrosities built from plans published in a 1955 issue of *Home Woodbutcher*. Well, plywood kayaks have

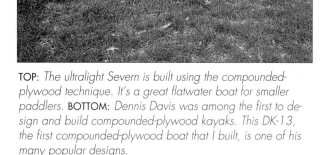

come a long way since those days. Flip through this book; I think you'll agree that plywood kayaks can be quite graceful.

Most plywood kayaks are of *hard-chine* design, like the Chesapeake models. That is, their hulls are composed of relatively flat panels joined at an angle. Hard-chine designs have several advantages over round-bottomed boats: they are well suited to heavy loads; they have high initial stability, which is nice on long trips; and the chines help in "carving" turns. Additionally, they are very straightforward to build.

TOP: *The ultralight Severn is built using the compounded-plywood technique. It's a great flatwater boat for smaller paddlers.* BOTTOM: *Dennis Davis was among the first to design and build compounded-plywood kayaks. This DK-13, the first compounded-plywood boat that I built, is one of his many popular designs.*

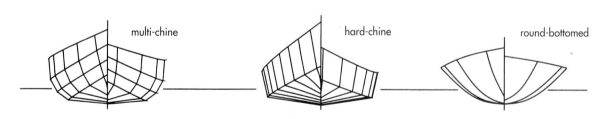

Cross sections of multi-chine, hard-chine, and round-bottomed hulls.

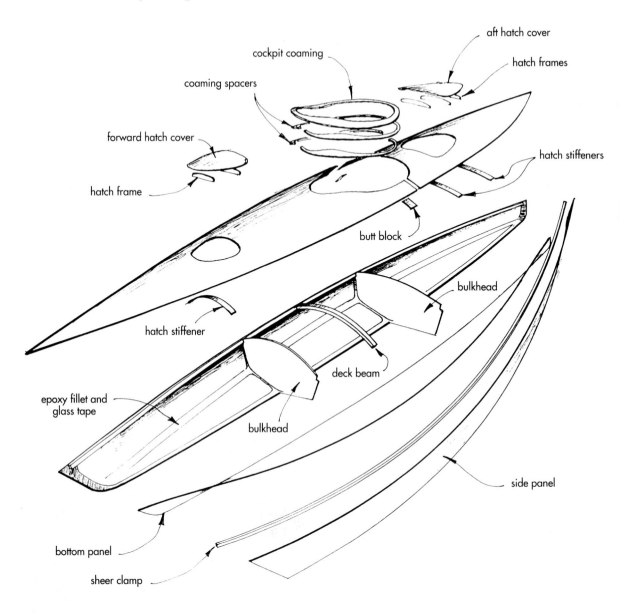

The parts and pieces of a wooden kayak.

Some paddlers like the feel of *multi-chine* kayaks like the West River 180. These paddlers are willing to trade some of the hard-chine kayak's handling characteristics for slightly better efficiency. Multi-chine boats have hulls composed of 6, 8, or 10 panels; they are, in effect, round-bottomed boats. A multi-chine hull has about 3 percent less wetted-surface area than a hard-chine hull with the same dimensions; this decreases resistance by about 1–2 percent. On the other hand, many paddlers feel that multi-chine kayaks don't handle or surf as well as those with hard-chine hulls. Initial stability of multi-chine hulls is often a bit lower than that of hard-chine hulls, and turns require more lean. Multi-chine boats are more difficult and more time-consuming to build because they have many more parts. Since they have many seams, considerable fiberglass work is required, but building one is still within the capabilities of most folks.

For ultimate efficiency, however, nothing moves like a round-bottomed boat. Most true round-bottomed plywood kayaks, like the Severn, are built using a technique variously called compounded plywood, bent plywood, stressed plywood, developed plywood, and, most descriptively, tortured plywood. This method was pioneered in the early 1960s by catamaran builders and by the kayak designer Dennis Davis. *Compounded-plywood* construction involves bending thin plywood in two planes simultaneously, producing a compound curve. It might be thought of as a modern version of the method used to build birchbark canoes. Compounded-plywood boats can have very pleasing rounded forms sometimes described as "organic."

Modern plywood kayaks, whether hard-chine, multi-chine, or round-bottomed, rarely need frames. This contributes to their light weight and simplicity. They are *monocoque* structures, meaning that they rely primarily on their skins, rather than on internal members, for strength. Many plywood kayaks, including all of my designs, can be constructed without forms or jigs, over which the hull is built. Today's plywoods bend so easily and consistently that special bending methods such as steam bending or soaking the wood aren't necessary.

The durability of modern wooden boats is due largely to the use of epoxy. When epoxy resin is mixed with a hardener, it becomes a tenacious adhesive that solidifies into a hard clear plastic. Brushed onto the wood's surface, epoxy penetrates into the wood's fibers and forms a tough skin that prevents the passage of water and fungus spores, which can cause wood to rot.

The Skills You Will Need

I teach several weeklong classes in kayak building each year. Many of my students have had absolutely no woodworking experience, yet they go home with fine boats.

A boatbuilding course is a great way to build a kayak in only one week even if you're a novice woodworker.

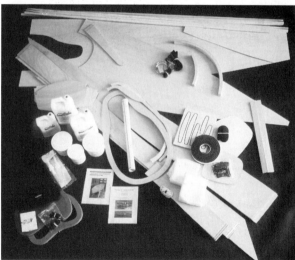

TOP: *Not a bad week's work. These students had just completed the WoodenBoat School course in St. Michaels, Maryland.* BOTTOM: *Kayak kits are a great way for novice woodworkers to build fine boats. This kit for a Patuxent kayak was manufactured by Chesapeake Light Craft.*

You certainly don't need to be an expert woodworker to build a kayak. In fact, most of the necessary skills can be learned in a few hours. You must know how to use a handsaw, a block plane, a drill, and a few other basic tools. You must also be able to measure and use a carpenter's square. Perhaps the hardest skill to learn is the patience to slow down every once in a while, stand back, and make sure everything is going as you intend.

If you have no woodworking experience, if your time is limited, or if you want to improve your skills quickly, attend a kayak building or boatbuilding class. Several boatbuilding schools offer courses in kayak building; in most you'll actually build your own boat during the course. The best-known of these is the WoodenBoat School in Brooklin, Maine, the self-proclaimed "wooden boat capital of the world." The campus is located on a beautiful waterfront estate that is also home to the offices of *WoodenBoat* and *Professional Boatbuilder* magazines. During the weeklong courses most students stay and dine at the school; in the evenings they enjoy the use of the school's fleet of classic wooden boats to go sailing or to paddle or row to one of the offshore islands. Wouldn't that be a nice way to spend a vacation?

You might also look into local boatbuilding clubs. There's a strong network of woodworkers and wooden boat builders in many parts of the country. For many years I belonged to a traditional small-boat association whose membership included three professional wooden boat builders and two naval architects who were usually willing to dispense free advice to fellow members. In addition, our club held demonstrations of building techniques, on-the-water rallies,

All types of kayaks are available in plan or kit form. This Mill Creek 13 can be paddled or sailed.

and talks by both amateur and professional boatbuilders. I could even borrow a tool I needed from some of the other members. Maritime museums are a good source of information on such clubs and other boatbuilding programs.

The hardest part of building your own kayak is getting started. By opening this book you've done that. But before you take saw to wood, read the entire book. Knowing what comes next can save you substantial time and trouble when you're building.

CHAPTER TWO

The Design

Kayaks are among the simplest of boats, yet thousands of kayak designs have been created, each of them someone's idea of the perfect boat. The first step in building a kayak is choosing a design or drawing your own. If you're an experienced kayaker, you probably know exactly what you want. You may even be able to judge how a boat will paddle just from looking at it. But novice paddlers need to do some research.

If you're not experienced, first decide what you want to do in your new boat. Do you plan to make long trips along windy, exposed coastlines? If so, you'll need a sturdy boat and a lot of skill and experience. Perhaps you want to race or to cross train for another sport. If that's

Wooden boat shows and symposia on sea kayaking provide a chance to see and test-paddle all sorts of kayaks. Paddle as many boats as you can and see how far you can push them.

11

TOP: *Prototypes are still the key to successful designs. This is Chesapeake Light Craft's prototype shop.* BOTTOM: *Visiting a kit manufacturer's showroom allows you to see many designs side by side.*

the case, a long, narrow (and tippy) kayak is called for. If you like to fly fish and take photographs, as I do, look for a little more stability and maneuverability. If you plan to make camping trips to remote areas—one of the best uses for a sea kayak—you'll need a roomy and seaworthy design. And if you simply want to get out on the water for an afternoon, a fairly stable, all-around sea kayak is just the thing. In any case, take every opportunity to paddle different boats before selecting one to build.

Knowing a little about how kayak, paddler, and water interact and about the elements of a kayak's design will help you make a wise choice. Kayak design is not a science; it's a blend of art, intuition, and engineering. This becomes obvious to me every time I launch a new design. Whether I've drawn the boat or built it to someone else's design, I am always surprised by some aspect of its performance. Still, if you combine experience and theory, you'll have a pretty good shot at choosing the boat that's right for you.

Length

Length is usually the first dimension to look at. To a large degree a kayak's length determines how fast it can go, how stable it is, and how much it will hold. Actually, two separate lengths must be considered for every boat. The first is the length overall, or *LOA*, which is the distance between the two most distant points on the bow and stern. The more important length is the length on the waterline, or *LWL*, which is the distance between the *immersed* ends of a kayak carrying a normal load.

Most benefits of length derive from a long LWL, not a long LOA. A boat with a LOA much longer than its LWL is said to have long overhangs. Long overhanging bows and sterns are often added to a design for cosmetic reasons. Some paddlers feel that long overhanging bows are beneficial in rough waters. But similar advantages can be achieved with a moderate overhang by increasing the volume in the bow. Long overhangs, particularly if they are overly upswept, can add considerable lateral surface area, making a boat more difficult to handle in strong winds.

Most paddlers know that a boat's top speed is related to its length. A boat creates a bow wave where it cuts through the water and a stern wave as the water comes together again at the boat's end; in order for waves to move faster they must be farther apart. A boat's theoretical top speed, or *hull speed*, in knots (a knot is 1.15 mph)

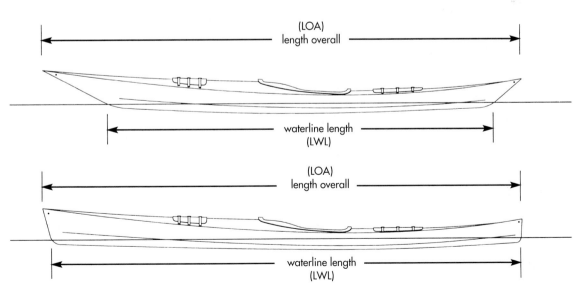

Waterline length (LWL) is not the same as length overall (LOA).

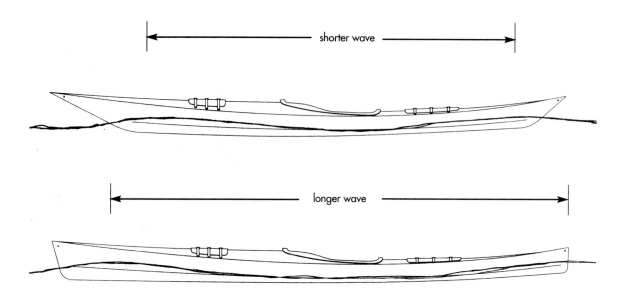

shorter wave

longer wave

Waterline length determines the distance between the bow wave and the stern wave, and thus the boat's speed.

is roughly 1.34 times the square root of the LWL. Now before you write to ask me to explain why Uncle Fred's 17-foot speedboat goes 50 knots while your 17-foot sea kayak goes 5 knots, let me explain that this rule doesn't apply to high-powered boats that plane on the surface of the water—I can't explain those boats. Actually, a kayak can attain very high speeds for brief periods when surfing down waves. Even on flat water, a kayak, like many boats with very narrow hulls, is capable of speeds slightly higher than its theoretical hull speed.

The importance of length in determining speed is often overemphasized. A paddler can only exert about one-quarter horsepower, so the limiting factor becomes overall drag that your available power must overcome and not the theoretical hull speed. Once the kayak's LWL approaches 17 feet or so, you'll gain little or no speed by lengthening it, unless you are a very powerful paddler. It's true that

racing kayaks can have a 20-foot LWL, but most of us rarely paddle fast enough to achieve hull speed in our kayaks. In fact, the extra wetted-surface area of the long hull increases the effort required at lower speeds.

But there's more to be gained from length than just speed. If you compare two kayaks that have different lengths but are otherwise similar in design, you'll find that the longer boat has several advantages over the shorter one. The longer boat won't pitch as violently in steep waves, and it will be more stable. It will have a higher volume and will hold more gear. And the longer boat will *track*, or go in a straight line, better. On the other hand, comparing the same two kayaks, the longer boat is less maneuverable, requires more materials to build, and is heavier and more expensive. Finally, the longer boat is harder to store and transport. Single sea kayaks with a LWL of 15 to 18 feet seem ideal. Double sea kayaks with a LWL of 17 to 21 feet work best. Flatwater kayaks are typically shorter, as are very wide kayaks.

Beam and Cross Section

After length you'll look at a kayak's beam, or width. Beam, like length, affects a kayak's volume, stability, and speed. The beam at both the waterline and overall should be considered. Closely related to beam is the cross-sectional shape of the kayak's hull. It may be round-bottomed, V-bottomed, flat-bottomed, or a combination of these shapes.

Wider boats are generally thought to be more stable. This is often, though not always, true. There are two elements of stability: *initial* and *ultimate* (sometimes called secondary). Initial stability is the type found in a rowboat or a flat-bottomed kayak with a wide waterline beam. A boat with high initial stability doesn't feel tippy, or *tender*, but if it's leaned too far it capsizes without warning. A boat with high ultimate stability, such as a kayak

The kayak on the left has less initial stability and less volume than the boat on the right. However, it also has a lower wetted-surface area.

with high, flared hull sides, may be tender at first, but as it starts to heel over, more of the hull is immersed and its resistance to capsizing increases. This initial tenderness actually helps a skilled paddler control the boat by allowing it to be easily leaned when turning and when in rough seas. Round- and V-bottomed boats and boats with narrow waterline beams

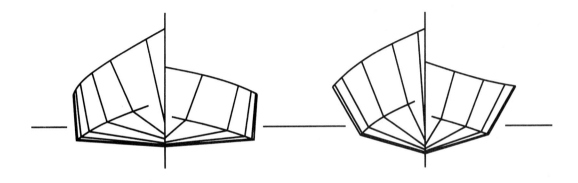

The boat on the left has high initial stability and low secondary stability. The hull on the right will exhibit low initial stability but high secondary stability.

usually have lower initial stability. Boats with flared sides and high volume tend to have high ultimate stability.

A good way to increase the stability of any boat is not to increase the beam but to lower the boat's center of gravity. Lowering a kayak's seat an inch or two can result in a dramatic increase in stability. All the weight in a kayak should be placed as low as possible, including the kayak's and your seat.

Shorter kayaks must be wider so that they can hold their intended cargo, which makes them less efficient at higher speeds. Beamy kayaks are usually slower than narrower boats. In addition, a normal-length paddle may strike the gunwales of a wide kayak. Wide kayaks sometimes don't track well, and they may be unattractive if the designer simply tries to widen and shorten an existing design. For single sea kayaks a beam of 21–25 inches is reasonable, as it can provide sufficient initial stability for comfortable touring yet is narrow enough that the boat can be Eskimo rolled. Doubles may be as wide as 36 inches since they will not be rolled. Recreational flatwater kayaks can be still wider, say, 30 inches for a single and 40 inches for a double.

Though the long, skinny boat on the left is obviously faster than the short, wide boat on the right, the shorter boat may actually be easier to paddle at low to medium speeds. It's interesting that both boats have approximately the same volume and burden, or carrying capacity.

Wetted-Surface Area

The wetted-surface area is the surface area of the hull that is below the waterline. At low speeds the friction of the hull's skin is a greater source of resistance to forward progress than the waves formed by the hull's forward motion. Thus, a long narrow boat with a high theoretical hull speed but a high wetted surface will require more energy to paddle at low speed than a short fat boat with a minimal wetted surface. Paddlers sometimes buy long kayaks because they think they will be able to go faster; for short bursts they will, but at normal touring speeds they may actually end up moving slower than they would have in a shorter boat with a lower wetted-surface area.

Boats with a very low wetted-surface area have a cross section resembling a semicircle; these hulls have a very low initial stability. In extreme cases, such as flatwater racing kayaks, only expert paddlers can handle them. Touring kayak hulls must be flattened out to increase the initial stability, and with it, the wetted-surface area. Hard-chine and flat-bottomed boats may have a slightly higher wetted surface than multi-chine or round-bottomed kayaks. The former, however, also tend to have a larger load-carrying capacity and handle better, which may be more important on long trips.

Prismatic Coefficient and Hull Form

Another measurement related to a boat's beam and cross section is its prismatic coefficient, or C_p. A kayak's C_p describes how full or fine-ended the hull is. In a boat with a high C_p the volume is distributed along the length, causing the ends to have a "full" shape. In a boat with a low C_p the volume is concentrated near the center and the ends are finely tapered. The C_p is the ratio between the volume of displacement (how much water a loaded boat displaces) and the volume of a prism that has

the same length as the LWL and the same cross-sectional area as the widest part of the submerged portion of the hull.

Most kayaks have a C_p of between 0.48 and 0.56. The importance of this number is that a boat with very full ends, and thus a high C_p, tends to "push" its bow and stern waves farther apart and toward the ends of the hull. And the farther apart the waves are, the faster the boat can move. Of course, when the C_p is too high, the waves become too big, and too much energy is required to push them; we then have a barge. A kayak with very fine ends, and thus a low C_p, doesn't make efficient use of its length to achieve a high hull speed because the bow and stern waves are too close together; however, such a boat may be very efficient at low and medium speeds. In the past, many designers didn't actually calculate a kayak's C_p; instead they relied on experience and a good eye to draw the proper balance between fullness and fineness in the ends. But today's computer design programs make short work of calculating and fine-tuning this and other coefficients.

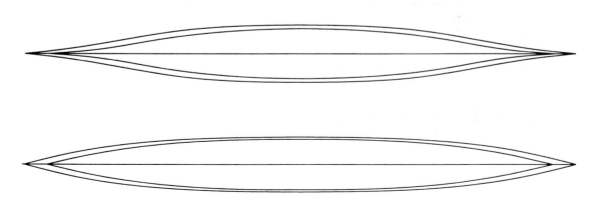

The waterline shapes of boats with low (top) and high (bottom) prismatic coefficients.

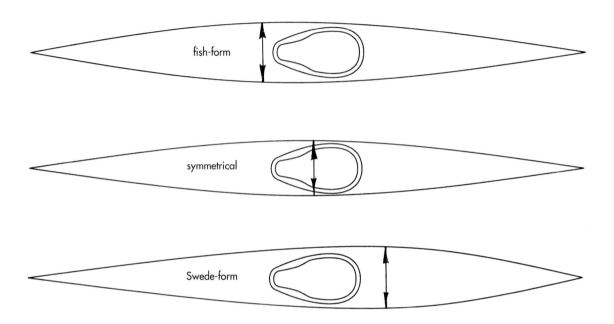

If the maximum beam is forward, the hull is said to be fish-form. If the maximum beam is amidships, it is symmetrical. A Swede-form boat has its widest point aft.

A kayak's ends must also have enough buoyancy to stay above water. When boats with a low C_p are paddled in steep waves, their ends may tend to dig into the face of the waves. This may result in broaching when paddling downwind, and it makes the boat difficult to control in other circumstances. In such boats the hull should flare, thus increasing the volume above the waterline and increasing reserve buoyancy.

The designer must also decide where to place the boat's maximum beam. If the widest part of the kayak is at or near the midpoint of its length, the boat is said to have a *symmetrical form*. If the maximum beam is forward of the midpoint, it has a *fish-form* hull; if it is aft of center, the boat has a *Swede-form* hull.

Fish-form and symmetrical hulls are thought to be more efficient than Swede-form hulls, but the difference, if any, is slight. Many modern kayaks appear to be Swede-form. Because a boat's bow overhang is usually much longer than its stern overhang, the maximum waterline beam of a symmetrical-form boat may be aft of the center of its overall length, causing it to appear to be a Swede-form. Some designers prefer to place the maximum beam aft of the cockpit so that the paddle will more easily clear the deck. Also, many paddlers seem to prefer the appearance of a Swede-form boat.

Volume

A kayak's volume is sometimes expressed in gallons or in cubic feet, but more often it is described as simply high, medium, or low. A kayak's length, beam, C_p, and *depth*—or deck height—influence volume. A high-volume kayak is one that will hold tons of gear and a big paddler. For long-distance touring you'll need sufficient space for packing camping gear and supplies. A high-volume boat is usually slower and heavier than a low- or medium-volume boat, but it is also drier and more comfortable. In strong winds, a high-volume kayak, with its higher bulk out of the water, will be more difficult to control than a lower-profile, lower-volume boat.

Having a boat that's matched to your weight, including the weight of the gear that you plan to carry, is very important. One of the easiest ways to improve your paddling performance is to choose a boat that's a good fit. A boat that's too small for you will sit too low in the water and will be difficult to control and turn. It will feel sluggish and slow, and waves will continually wash the deck. Too large a boat will be blown about on windy days and may

not track well; it may also weathercock, broach, and be more difficult to roll.

One of the advantages of building your own kayak is that you can choose a model that's a perfect fit. Since the manufacturers of plastic boats have small fortunes tied up in their molds, they may claim that a particular model will fit paddlers weighing from 100 to 250 pounds. But a good kayak should fit a fairly narrow weight range—50 to 75 pounds. A wooden boat designer, whose mold consists of sheets of paper or a computer file, can design a boat in three sizes to cover that 100- to 250-pound weight range.

Rocker

Rocker is the upward curve of the kayak's keel line over its length. If you place a kayak with pronounced rocker, such as a whitewater kayak, on a flat floor, its middle will touch the floor, while its ends (at the waterline) will be several inches above

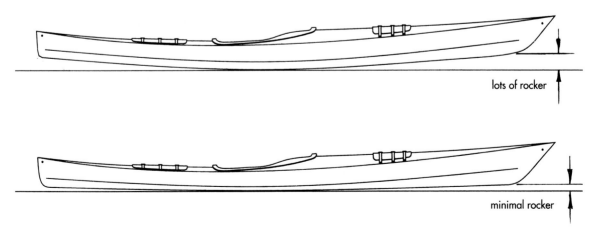

lots of rocker

minimal rocker

Rocker affects a boat's wetted-surface area, handling, and speed.

it. Such a boat turns easily but is difficult to paddle in a straight line. A boat with no rocker placed on the same floor will touch the floor over most of its length, which means it will be difficult to turn but easy to paddle straight. *Tracking*, or holding a straight course despite the effects of wind and waves, is more important than turning ability in touring and sea kayaks. To strike a balance between tracking and turning, most sea kayaks are designed with a small amount of rocker—1 to 3 inches. Longer boats, boats with V-shaped hulls, and boats with very fine ends can have more rocker without compromising tracking. Rocker improves a boat's handling in waves. A common misconception is that adding rocker makes a boat slower; actually, modern flatwater racing kayaks often have considerable rocker.

Balance

Sailors often describe boats as having *weather helm* or *lee helm*. These terms describe the boat's tendency, when steered in a straight course across the wind, to turn into the wind or away from it. In kayaks these tendencies can make paddling difficult or even dangerous. Most kayaks tend to *weathercock*, or turn into the wind. Since facing into the wind and waves is the easiest way to ride out rough conditions, weathercocking can be considered a safety feature. Should you become incapacitated or exhausted, your boat will face the weather and perhaps allow you time to rest or recover. Unfortunately, some kayaks weathercock so severely that they are difficult to paddle in any but the

mildest winds unless they are fitted with a rudder or skeg. A very few kayaks tend to turn downwind, which is dangerous; I would not paddle further from shore than I could swim in such a craft.

Drawing a boat with just the right balance is one of the tougher challenges a kayak designer faces. The problem is one of aiming at a moving target—as wind conditions, speed through the water, and paddler weight change, so does the balance of the boat. The designer must try to draw a boat that will be well balanced in most conditions even though it may not be perfect in any.

Rudders and Skegs

Bring up the subject of rudders with a group of sea kayakers and you'll hear some extreme opinions. "Real men (or women) don't need no stinkin' rudders; and it's harder to roll if the footbraces slide; the Inuit didn't have rudders," one camp might say. Another might not be so vehement: "I remember that trip in Baja; we had wind off the stern quarter for three days straight. Sure was nice to have a rudder then." It is the long-distance touring paddler who most appreciates rudders.

In heavy winds and seas, rudders are invaluable. Even the best-balanced boat may weathercock severely in some conditions, and all kayaks will tend to broach in steep, quartering seas. These traits are not difficult to correct for a few hours—a few extra paddle strokes on one side, a lean and a sweep—but try to keep it up for a whole day or a week and your downwind arm will throb from the effort. Rudders are especially useful in doubles and in heavily loaded singles.

Any kayak that must rely on a rudder for proper handling is unsafe. Rudders shouldn't be a remedy for a poorly designed hull. Though rudders have become far more reliable in recent years, they can and do fail; they should be considered a convenience, not an essential.

A fixed or adjustable skeg can also be used to balance a boat in rough conditions. A skeg is a small fin under the stern that aids in tracking, much like the feathers on an arrow. Adding a skeg to a boat that is not designed to track well, such as a whitewater kayak, will greatly improve handling in non-whitewater conditions. On a sea kayak a fixed skeg can aid tracking too much, making maneuvering difficult. In this case a skeg that retracts into a trunk in the hull can be fitted. This ad-justable skeg is lowered or raised using a line or wire cable led to the cockpit. Its advantage is that it will change the boat's balance and aid in tracking without the complexity of a rudder or sliding foot-braces and only to the degree desired by the paddler. But skegs are not as efficient as rudders, and skeg trunks take up a fair amount of cargo room. For the long-distance paddler the rudder is the better option.

Deck and Cockpit

The deck is an integral part of a kayak's design. It adds enormous rigidity and strength to the hull. The deck must have sufficient *camber*, or curvature, to accommodate the paddler's knees, feet, and gear. Camber increases a kayak's volume and

Cambered decks are stronger than flat or multipanel decks, look nicer, and are easier to make.

allows the deck to shed water quickly, keeping the paddler drier. A kayak with a cambered or peaked forward deck is easier to Eskimo roll. However, decks that are too high increase windage and make the boat more difficult to handle in extreme weather conditions. A high aft deck may hinder leaning back to roll.

A few plywood kayak decks are composed of flat, as opposed to cambered, sections. Such decks often have a tendency to flex or "oil-can." Most are designed in the mistaken belief that they are easier to build than curved decks, but cambered decks are often simpler to construct and are usually lighter and stronger.

A kayak's cockpit must fit the paddler; it must be both snug and comfortable. The cockpit opening should allow the paddler to enter and exit the boat quickly and efficiently. It must not be so wide or long, however, that the paddler can't brace his or her knees under the deck. A keyhole-shaped cockpit is often used because it can be long enough to allow easy entry and exit while still providing a place to brace one's knees.

A sea kayak's coaming must be strong enough and low enough to sit on when performing a wet reentry. If the kayak is to be used primarily in calm water without a sprayskirt, then the coaming may be higher to help keep the paddler dry. Since wet reentries are rare in such conditions, the coaming need not be so beefy.

Choosing a Design

As you consider a design, remember that any design is a compromise. It's relatively easy to design a boat that's well suited to one specific purpose—a very fast boat, for example, or a boat capable of carrying heavy loads. But designing a boat that can do several things well is an art.

By comparing elements of a new design to those of kayaks you've paddled, you'll get a fair idea of how it will suit you. But don't get hung up on "numbers"—you'll never notice an extra inch or two of length or an extra half-inch of rocker. If the design is 90 percent right, build it and go paddling.

All else aside, I've found that prettier boats are better boats. If you look at a new design and it doesn't move you—if it won't bring a smile to your face whenever you see it sitting on the beach—then it isn't the boat for you.

Should You Build from Plans or from a Kit?

Because of the quality and availability of modern precut kayak kits, it can be difficult to decide whether to start your new kayak from a set of plans or from a kit. In most cases, buying a kit costs about 20 percent more than ordering the plans and materials to build a boat, so you might save $100 to $150 by building a kayak from scratch. You might save a bit more by buying all the supplies locally, eliminating the shipping costs, but unless you live in a large city in the Northeast or Northwest, chances are you'll end up ordering at least some of the materials. Most likely you'd still end up ordering the marine-grade mahogany plywood or paying much more for it at a local distributor.

There are many advantages to building from a kit. The parts are all precut so you'll save a lot of building time. You won't need to learn to cut scarf joints. The deck beams are prelaminated. One thing you might not have considered is that a lot of "confidence" comes with a kit. You know the pieces are properly cut, so you shouldn't have any of those nagging doubts: "That part looks funny—I hope I cut it right." But time is still the reason that most amateur builders choose kits and that many professional kayak builders, when building boats for clients, start with a kit.

A kit is not always the way to go, however. If your goal is to get your boat launched as quickly as possible, or if you have limited free time, then you probably should start from a kit. On the other hand, many designs are simply not available in kit form. And if you want to learn as much as possible about the process of boatbuilding, then you should start from plans. Many builders enjoy building these boats just as much as paddling them—it's a lot of fun to start with a few sheets of paper and end up with a boat. For these builders, a kit simply eliminates some of the fun.

Plans

One of the great pleasures of boatbuilding is deciding which boat to build. You can spend many happy hours looking through plan and kit catalogs, back issues of *WoodenBoat* magazine, *Sea Kayaker*, and *Messing about in Boats*, and designers' websites. But sooner or later it's time to send off a check and open the kit box and/or unroll your plans. If you're new to boatbuilding, the plans may seem complicated and confusing. But most boat plans are drawn in a similar style, and once you get the hang of reading one set of them, reading most others will be as easy as reading this book.

READING PLANS

Traditionally, a set of plans for a small boat offers three views: *profile*, showing the boat from the side; *half breadth*, or *deck plan*, showing the boat from the top; and *body plan*, or *sections*, showing a combination front-and-back view. A set of lines resembling the contour lines on a map, and serving the same purpose, may be superimposed over these views; these are descriptively called the boat's lines. Boatbuilders traditionally measure and scale up these lines to full size using a process called *lofting*. Many designers also include a table of measurements from the centerline to the edge of the hull at particular cross sections. These cross sections are called *stations*, and the table is called the *table of offsets*. Offsets make the job of lofting far easier and faster.

Now if all this has you considering taking up bowling instead of kayak building, I have some good news. Most kayak plans drawn for amateur builders contain measurements for all the parts and don't require lofting or using tables of offsets. Many even include full-size patterns for parts such as seats, footbraces, bulkheads, and coamings. Still, it's important to study the boat's lines before you start building so that you'll know how the boat's hull should look.

In addition to the main views of the boat, there will also be a few expanded

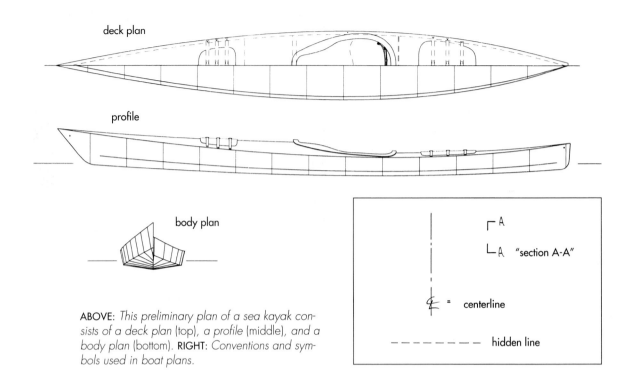

deck plan

profile

body plan

┌ A
└ A   "section A-A"

⌀ = centerline

— — — — — — — hidden line

ABOVE: *This preliminary plan of a sea kayak consists of a deck plan* (top), *a profile* (middle), *and a body plan* (bottom). **RIGHT:** *Conventions and symbols used in boat plans.*

views in the plans, which show additional details. These close-ups should be self-explanatory and are critical to understanding how the pieces of the boat go together. There will usually be sketches of the seat, hatches, footbraces, and other little parts that would only crowd the primary views.

In addition to the plan sheets you'll need the *scantlings* and/or the bill of materials. The scantlings detail the materials from which the parts of the boat are made, and the bill of materials lists all the materials you'll need. On kayak plans both lists may be combined, or the scantlings may be incorporated into the building directions. Study the bill of materials carefully so that you can estimate that other important bill: your bill *for* materials.

Occasionally, you'll see plans with full-size patterns for hull panels; stay away from these. Modern printing methods are simply not accurate enough to produce inexpensive scale drawings in the 8- to 20-foot-long sheets required. By the time the end of the sheet of paper has passed through the printer's rollers, the drawing might be distorted by several inches. When Chesapeake Light Craft tried publishing full-size patterns for my designs, angry builders called to say that their panels didn't fit well. Experienced builders said that it was far more time-consuming to crawl around on the floor tracing 16-foot panels than to simply lay them out using scale plans.

Reproduced in chapter 5 are the plans for three kayaks. These plans, like most plans published in books and magazines, are reduced from full size to fit on these pages; thus, some detail is lost. When you decide to build a particular kayak, you should invest in a full set of plans from the designer or plans catalog. It's certainly possible to build boats from plans reproduced in books and magazines, but having the full-size set and accompanying instructions will save you many hours and doubts, especially if you are a novice builder. The extra dollars you spend will be forgotten when the boat is finished.

Modifying Plans

Every paddler has his or her own idea of the perfect boat. An advantage of building your own boat is that you can accommodate your personal wants and needs. Modifications, if well thought out, will make your boat ideally suited to your paddling style. But before deciding on a design change, consider that a boat's designer has put substantial thought and experience into the design. Ask yourself whether the changes you are thinking about will affect the strength of the kayak. Will it still be as seaworthy? If you put in a larger cockpit, for example, will the boat lose rigidity? Can you find a sprayskirt to fit it? You may want a stronger boat and decide to increase the thickness of the hull skin, but the thicker wood might not conform to the desired hull shape. A better solution might be to add a second layer of fiberglass cloth over the bottom. If the changes you want to make seem major, or if you're unsure of the effect they will have on the boat's strength, write to the designer for advice.

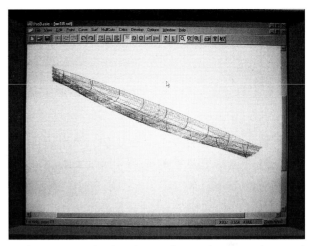

Today most wooden kayaks are designed using sophisticated computer programs.

Designing Your Own Kayak

Many experienced paddlers are capable of designing their own kayaks if they are willing to devote a fair amount of time and study to the task. If you choose to try your own design, consider starting with an existing design that you like and slowly redrawing it to better meet your needs. Designing from a blank sheet of paper is much more difficult; I wouldn't recommend trying it until you've built a few boats.

Computer design programs, which make computations and panel expansion far simpler, are ideal for designing kayaks. Several share-ware programs are powerful enough for the occasional kayak designer. The least expensive professional programs cost only a few hundred dollars, yet they can accomplish in seconds what required a full day at the drafting table only a few decades ago. If you decide to invest in a boat-design program, I can recommend

Ply-Boats as an easy-to-learn first program, and New Wave Software's Pro-Basic as a more capable but not overwhelming alternative. Remember that these programs are only tools; don't let the software manual fool you into thinking that owning a boat-design program will make you a boat designer. That would be like believing that a word-processing program will make you a writer.

Scale Models

So you've designed the perfect kayak or found the perfect design, but you wish you could see it before you devote all that time to building it. Scale models have been used by boat designers for almost as long as boats have been designed. In fact, a traditional way to design a boat is to carve half the hull to scale, called a *half model* or *half hull*, and then to take measurements from it when drawing the boat's lines. Even

though most designers now use three-dimensional computer-assisted design (CAD) programs to visualize new designs, many still like to see a wooden model if the design is complicated or a major departure from earlier work. Since you will be building a plywood kayak, it seems only logical to make a plywood model.

The plywood to use is ½-inch aircraft-grade birch. At a scale of 1 inch to 1 foot (a model of a 16-foot kayak would be 16 inches long), the ½-inch plywood bends to about the same degree as 3 mm or 4 mm plywood does on a full-size boat.

The solid wood pieces should be made of bass or other softwood. But the solid pieces will have to be a little thicker than the 1:12 scale calls for or they won't be strong enough to support the plywood.

Slow-drying cyanoacrylate glue, available at hobby shops, should be used to hold the parts together. Essentially a slow-drying superglue, it dries in 3 to 10 minutes. If you're in a hurry, buy some

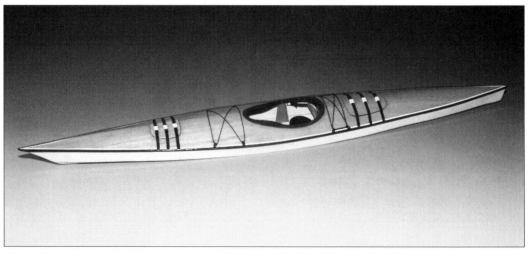

Boatbuilder and artist Carl Ulanowicz made this fine model of the Chesapeake 17 he was considering building. Satisfied with the shape and design, he completed two beautiful full-size versions.

accelerator to speed things up so that you won't have to spend all night holding tiny kayak parts together.

The fastest way to build a kayak model is to begin by taking your plans to a copy shop and having them reduced to a 1:12 scale. Then cut the pieces out of the copy and tape them to the ½-inch plywood. Use a pair of scissors to cut out the plywood parts and a razor knife and small saw to cut out the solid parts. Glue every-thing together just as you would when building a real boat. Use masking tape, paper clips, and alligator clips for clamps.

Building a model first will give you valuable insights into how to assemble the real boat and how the finished boat will look. Now carefully put your model away until it's time to varnish the full-size boat. Then take it out and use it to bribe the neighbor's kid to stay away until the var-nish is dry.

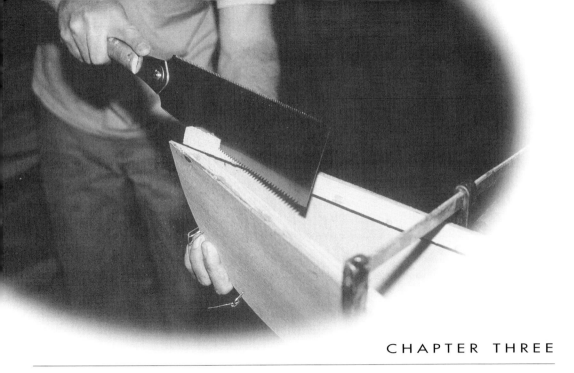

CHAPTER THREE

The Tools

At Hull Cove Tools on Mount Desert Island, Maine, there are shelves upon shelves of old tools. Boxes and racks of ancient planes, saws, spokeshaves, drills, bevel squares, clamps, and hammers fill every square foot of space. The shop smells of hardened steel, lubricating oil, and musty wood. I've spent happy hours combing the dusty recesses of each shelf and cabinet looking for hundred-year-old masterpieces ready to do duty again. I've wondered how many ships, houses, and boats these tools have created and how many they have still to build.

Most of the tools at Hull Cove are good tools. The cheap tools, the discount specials, the homeowner-quality tools have long since broken, bent, and rusted away.

The tools on these shelves are the keepers—the sort of tools used by shipwrights, carpenters, jointers, cabinetmakers, and farmers who couldn't afford to waste money on cheap tools. They are the sort of tools you should use to build your kayak.

Professional-quality tools are expensive and sometimes a challenge to find. But you'll need relatively few of them to build a kayak, so the extra cost isn't much. And when your kayak is finished, the tools will still have a lifetime or two of repairs and projects in them. In a few years their cost will be forgotten, but their quality and utility will be long appreciated by you, your children, and your grandchildren.

The differences between good tools and junk might be subtle—the type of

29

steel used, the quality of the finish, and the precision of the machining. Professional tools made by Stanley are of fine quality, as are brands such as Record, Marples, Kunz, Sandvik, Jorgensen, and Bacho. One indication of a tool's quality is its price and another is where you find it. A professional cabinetmaker's supply house, for example, is not likely to carry junk.

Professional-quality power tools cost two to four times as much as power tools designed for use by homeowners. But for their steep prices you'll get tools that stay adjusted, that you'll be able to find parts for, and that will probably last a lifetime. The only power tools you may need are a saber saw, a drill, and a small sander. Look for brands such as Porter Cable, DeWalt, Milwaukee, Fien, Makita, Bosch, AEG, and Hitachi, but be aware that many professional tool companies have introduced "homeowner" lines that aren't so well made.

As much as we may like to support local businesses, your local hardware store may not be the place to buy tools, nor should you always rely on the local home-improvement store, though some do carry a good selection. High-quality tools are tools made for professionals, so ask local boatbuilders, carpenters, or contractors where they buy their tools. You'll be pleased at how much you can learn and how much money you'll save by buying from a professional tool supplier. If you live in a small town where it's hard to find good tools, turn to some of the excellent mail-order discount tool companies that advertise in *WoodenBoat* or *Fine Woodworking* magazines.

A list of tools you'll need whether you are building a kayak from scratch or from a kit appears on pages 39–40. Most of these are readily available tools used by carpenters or cabinetmakers. If you're familiar with traditional boatbuilding, you may be surprised by how few tools are required to build plywood kayaks.

Tools for Measuring

Accurate measuring is critical to boatbuilding. The old adage "Measure twice, cut once" is never truer than when building boats. If your parts are measured accurately, they will go together with little trouble, but sloppily measured pieces will require fiddling, trimming, gap filling, and even swearing. The few minutes you saved by measuring hurriedly will mean many more wasted when it comes time to assemble.

Before you start building, check all your measuring tools against one another. It's not uncommon to find that a tape measure doesn't agree exactly with a yardstick. I make all critical distance measurements with my tape measure or my metal rule. I am certain that these are correct, so if there's any error I know who to blame.

The tool you'll use more than any other will be your tape measure. Stanley, Starrett, and Lufkin make the best ones. The most durable and easiest to use are the 25-foot models with blades 1 inch wide. The 30-foot models are also good, but their springs tend to wear out sooner. Short, thin tape measures are best left for hanging pictures and building birdhouses.

I use a metal rule divided into ½₄-inch marks for measuring critical thicknesses like scarf lines, fastener lengths, drill-bit diameters, and other small dimensions. I also have a set of vernier calipers for critical measuring, but I'll admit that they're really overkill. For laying out longer lines, you'll need a piece of thin string or a carpenter's chalkline.

In addition to tools for measuring distances, you'll need tools for measuring angles. A carpenter's square guarantees right angles when you lay out the kayak's hull and deck panels. If you don't already have one, buy the 24- by 18-inch version. A small, 6- by 9-inch try square is handy for laying out and checking right angles in close quarters. The traditional boatbuilder's adjustable, or bevel, square, is also very useful—I wouldn't be without one. If you need to trace the curve of a circle with a given radius, you can make a homemade compass with some string, a pencil, and a nail, but a set of *trammels*, which resemble a bar compass, makes the job easier.

If building from plans, you'll need a couple of *battens*, long thin strips of wood that bend in a smooth, or *fair*, curve. They are used to draw the curves in a boat's panels when transferring the measurements from a set of plans onto the plywood; think of them as flexible straightedges. Find or make a ¾-inch-

My measuring tools include a tape measure, a metal rule, a chalkline, a mechanical pencil, a bevel square, and a carpenter's square.

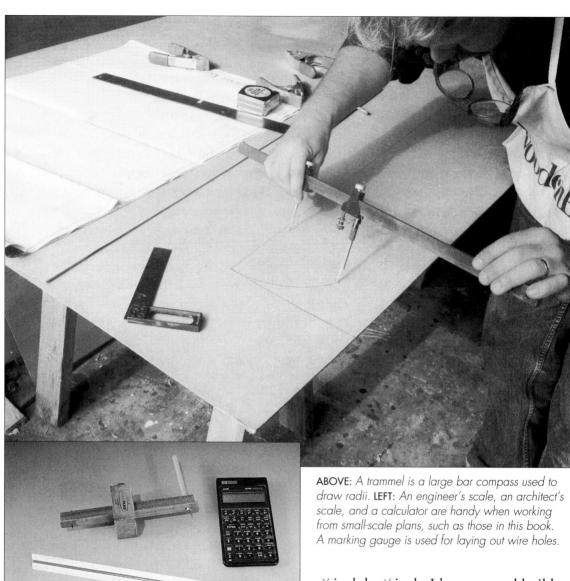

ABOVE: *A trammel is a large bar compass used to draw radii.* **LEFT:** *An engineer's scale, an architect's scale, and a calculator are handy when working from small-scale plans, such as those in this book. A marking gauge is used for laying out wire holes.*

square piece of flexible wood with straight grain and no knots, splits, or other imperfections. It should be at least 10 feet long, but 16 feet or longer is better. Find or make a second batten measuring about

¾ inch by ½ inch. I know several builders who use window molding from a home-improvement store as batten stock. Battens last a lifetime, so it's well worth searching the lumberyard for a nice piece of wood from which to rip a collection of battens varying in thickness and stiffness. At Chesapeake Light Craft we often used a metal batten that was nothing more that a 20-foot piece of square-section steel from the local welding shop. Such steel battens are inexpensive and make perfect curves.

Once you've made a measurement, you'll need to mark it. Some craftsmen use only a knife or a scribe to make the mark because they leave thinner lines than a pencil does. I prefer to use a sharp pencil because the line is easier to see. A draftsman's mechanical pencil is best because it never needs sharpening, but I'm always losing mine. A useful tool, though not essential, is a marking gauge. I use it to mark scarf lines and the position of the wire holes before stitching a hull together. Finally, an engineer's scale, an architect's scale, and a calculator might come in handy when working from some plans.

Tools for Cutting

In the first edition of this book I said that the only necessary power tool was a saber saw. I now think that you can use two Japanese handsaws to cut all the plywood parts for a kayak in a few hours.

Nonetheless, saber saws are nice to have. They fall into one of two categories: expensive, heavy-duty professional models and inexpensive, low-quality homeowner models. Though you certainly don't need the power of a professional model to cut the light materials you'll use for kayak building, the higher-quality construction and superior blade guides on professional models make them a better choice. I use a top-handle Porter Cable saber saw that I'm quite fond of; Bosch and Hitachi also make fine saber saws. Many boatbuilders

prefer saber saws without handles, called *barrel-grip models*, because they are a bit easier to control. Stay away from saws with a scroll feature because the scroll mechanism will eventually loosen and the blade will wander and twist. Be sure to buy a saber saw that has a blower to clear sawdust away from the blade so that you can see what you're cutting. Another essential feature is some sort of blade guide mounted on or just above the saw's baseplate. Without this feature the blade will tend to wander and bend as you cut through thick materials.

The best saber-saw blades are the bimetal type. They're often painted white, and they cost more than regular blades, but since you'll only wear out one or two blades per kayak, the additional cost is minimal. I use woodcutting blades with 10 teeth per inch.

A small handsaw is essential for accurate cuts in solid pieces, and it can also be used on plywood in place of a saber saw. My current favorite is a Japanese saw. Japanese saws cut on the pull stroke, so the blades can be much thinner than on a western saw, which cuts as you push. They also cut faster, leave a thinner kerf, and are easier to control. Of the many types of Japanese saws available, the most versatile is the *ryoba noko giri*, which has a flexible blade with crosscutting teeth along one side and ripping teeth along the other.

A small keyhole saw is also useful. Again I recommend a Japanese saw, particularly the type that looks like a steak knife, but was developed for trimming bonsai trees. This is an inexpensive saw that works well for trimming cockpit

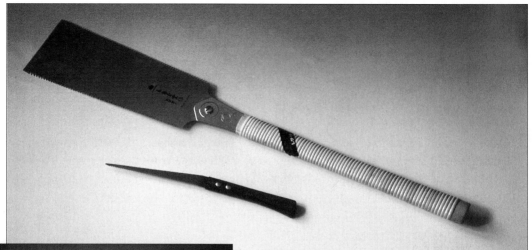

TOP: *I'm fond of saws made in Japan. At the top is my ryoba noko giri, which has teeth for both crosscutting and ripping. The tiny Japanese keyhole saw was originally designed for trimming bonsai trees, but it makes short work of trimming cockpit and hatch openings as well.* **BOTTOM:** *A saber saw is certainly useful but not essential. If you decide to buy one, consider only professional-quality models. The small circular saw on the right is another useful power tool. It makes much smoother cuts than those made with a saber saw.*

cutouts and hatch openings and for cutting sharp curves.

Sooner or later you have to face the fact that unless you're starting from a precut kit, you'll need to rip some parts from solid wood. The best saw for that job is a table saw. But unless you plan to build a lot more than one kayak, the cost of a table saw may be prohibitive. Instead, arrange to use a friend's table saw or pay a lumberyard to rip the sheer clamps and other solid wood pieces for you. Actually, with a bit of searching you might find pieces of the right size already cut at a lumberyard.

A circular saw is useful for cutting boards to length, splitting sheets of plywood, and even for cutting out hull panels that have only gentle curves. In fact, if you use a long straightedge as a guide, you can use a circular saw to do many of the tasks normally done on the table saw. I am most impressed by the tiny, 4½-inch-blade Porter Cable worm-drive trim saw. There are a number of rechargeable trim saws available, but the models I've tried don't have enough battery life.

Planes and Chisels

Woodworkers love planes, so you may be disappointed to learn that only a block plane is needed to build the kayaks in this

SHARPENING TOOLS

One of the first things I do when teaching a boat-building class is show my students how to sharpen their block planes and other edged tools. Watching a roomful of students struggling with dull tools is too much to bear; boatbuilding should be fun, and sharp, well-adjusted tools are a pleasure to use.

I prefer to sharpen tools on a Japanese water-stone. I think it is easier to use and leaves a better edge than an oilstone or Arkansas stone. A combination waterstone with a 1,000-grit surface on one side and a 6,000-grit surface on the other is perfect for sharpening woodworking tools or even kitchen knives. These stones use water as a lubricant and should be soaked for a few hours prior to use. I store my stone in a water-filled plastic container. Here I describe sharpening a plane's iron, or blade, but most tools are sharpened the same way.

First flatten the back; the back of the iron makes half the sharp edge, so this is important. Splash some water onto the coarse side of the stone and lay the iron on it, back face down. Sharpen the iron by pushing it up and down the stone in a circular motion. Use the entire stone, splash more water on it frequently, and check often to see if the back is smooth and flat. This may take some time if the tool is new; tool factories do a poor job of sharpening blades. When you see that the stone has made contact with the entire back of the iron (look at the sheen), sharpen for 3 more minutes on the fine side of the stone.

Now sharpen the front. Hold the blade against the coarse side of the stone so that it rests on its bevel. Rock the blade slightly to get a feel for when it's resting squarely on the bevel. Move the blade back and forth on the stone making a long oval circuit. Keep your fingers close to the bevel and press down gently. Make sure that the iron remains at a constant angle with the bevel flat on the stone. When the entire bevel has been sharpened (again, look at the sheen), repeat for 1 minute, or 20 up-and-down strokes, on the fine side. Now draw your fingernail down the back of the edge. You should feel a tiny burr, or "wire," made by the thin metal edge bent back in the sharpening process. Lay the blade on its back again and pull it down the stone once to remove the wire. Finally, dry the iron. If you did everything right, you could almost shave with this edge. Once the blade is true and sharp, sharpen it often; the process will take only a few minutes.

If you don't have the temperament to hand-sharpen tools and can afford an electric waterstone sharpener, don't hesitate to get one. My little Wen electric sharpener is one of my most appreciated tools.

Sharpening a plane's iron.

book. The block plane is likely to become your favorite tool. You'll use it to cut scarfs, to trim hull and deck panels, to clean up rough edges, and to shape small parts.

Block planes are available in standard models with an angle of about 20 degrees between the blade and the work surface and in low-angle models with an angle of 12½ degrees. The low-angle type is better suited to the cross-grain planing usually required in kayak building. The standards are the Stanley model 60½ low-angle plane and the similar but slightly nicer Record 60½. If you already own a standard block plane, there's no need to buy a low-angle type; I used an old Stanley model 220 for years until I dropped and cracked it. If you are an accomplished woodworker, or plan to be, look into the three block planes made by Lie-Nielsen. They are the most perfect—and most expensive—planes I've ever used. Beautifully machined and polished, they are as much works of art as they are tools. If you try one, you'll end up buying it, just as I did—you've been warned.

You could certainly build a kayak without any chisels, but given their usefulness and low cost, it would be false economy. A ½- or ¾-inch cabinetmaker's chisel is all you'll need. If you keep it very sharp, you'll often use it to trim pieces for that perfect fit. In addition to my good chisels, I have a set of cheap chisels that I use for scraping off glue and other tasks that would ruin my good ones.

Staplers

OK, a stapler is not a traditional boatbuilder's tool, but when you need to clamp large, awkward plywood pieces temporarily, no other tool is as useful. If

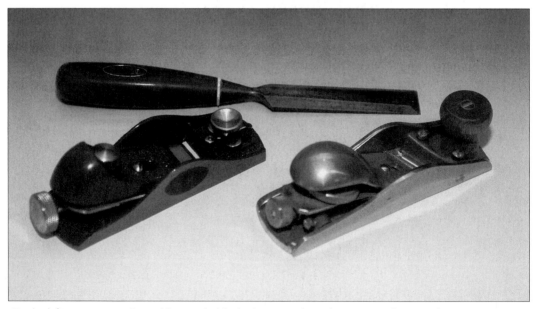

On the left is a very nice Record low-angle block plane. On the right is a magnificent and very expensive Lie-Nielsen plane. A couple of chisels are also useful.

you fill it with stainless steel, Monel, or bronze staples, they can be left in place. If you think that the staples will spoil the finish, they are easy to remove, and the tiny holes they leave are easy to fill. My stapler is an Arrow T-50 filled with ⅜-inch stainless steel staples.

Clamps

To build the kayaks in this book, you'll need a lot of clamps; twenty-five would not be too many. Most of your clamps can be old-fashioned C-clamps. Operations requiring the most clamps—gluing in the sheer clamps and the cockpit coaming—can be accomplished with small, 2-inch C-clamps. These can be bought very cheaply from professional tool-supply companies, so there's no excuse for running out. A few 2-inch spring clamps are also nice to have around for those times when you've only one free hand. Light-duty bar clamps, like the popular orange Jorgensens, are the most useful large clamps. Every boatbuilder should own a couple of the 6-inch and 18-inch ones. With practice, they can be operated with one hand.

If you're really strapped for cash, or just cheap, you can make effective clamps from schedule-40 plastic drainpipe. Get a length of 4-inch-diameter pipe and slice it into 1- to 2-inch rings. Split each ring, and you'll have spring clamps with enough clamping pressure for most epoxy joints.

Oil or wax the clamp's threads so they won't become fouled with epoxy. You'll often need a clamp in a hurry, so

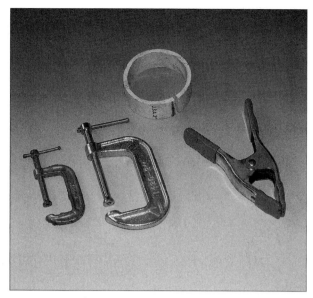

You can never have too many clamps. The little C-clamps on the left are inexpensive and most useful. A few spring clamps, such as the one on the right, are handy when you have only one free hand. Homemade spring clamps can be fashioned from schedule-40 PVC plumbing pipe.

hang them all from a shelf or horizontal bar within easy reach of your work area. There are few things more frustrating than trying to untangle a pile of clamps while your carefully aligned parts slide apart.

Sanders

Sanding, like taxes, is one of the unpleasant realities of life. Compared with cold-molded or strip-planked boats, plywood kayaks don't require much sanding. You could do all that's required by hand in a day. Still, most of us will choose to use an electric sander.

Today's small random-orbital sanders have eliminated much of the tedium of sanding. They sand quickly and don't leave swirl marks. The better models have

TOP: *On the right is a Bosch random-orbital sander that's both powerful and comfortable to use. My reliable old Makita quarter-sheet finishing sander is slower, but it does the same job.* BOTTOM: *A rechargeable drill is handy.*

sanders is the quarter-sheet Makita palm sander. Many other companies make similar models, but the Makita fits your hand just right. It sands fast enough for you to see progress but not so fast that you'll accidentally sand through layers of plywood or fiberglass tape. Quarter-sheet sanders use inexpensive sheet sandpaper rather than costly hook-and-loop pads.

In addition to an electric sander, you'll need a sanding block. The only type to get is the flexible solid rubber block that takes a quarter-width strip of sandpaper. 3M makes these, but less expensive imitations are available.

effective dust-removal systems. Hook-and-loop pads make quick work of changing paper. I'm most impressed with the Bosch and Porter Cable sanders.

If you don't mind a slightly slower machine, one of the best inexpensive

Drills

You can get by with almost any drill, including an old-fashioned eggbeater type. I use a rechargeable professional model with a clutch. You don't need much drilling power to build these kayaks, so cordless drills are fine. In fact, they're almost addictive. The clutch is useful when driving screws because it prevents them from being overdriven. On the other hand, inexpensive plug-in drills are always better than cheap rechargeable models.

You'll need a set of drill bits. Cheap drill bits bend, break, and get dull quickly. Instead, consider a small but high-quality set of brad-point bits. Buy an extra ¹⁄₁₆-inch bit because that's the size you'll use for wire-tie holes.

Miscellaneous Tools

Other tools you'll need include a set of screwdrivers, a pair of pliers, a pair of side-cutters, a small hammer for driving ring nails (if you plan to use them), and a pair of scissors. A tool you may not need but is handy to have is a wooden mallet for tapping your chisel. Finally, don't start work until you have a pair of safety glasses and a respirator.

Tool List

Tools you'll need for building from a precut kit:

- Tape measure
- 12-inch metal rule
- Carpenter's square
- String line or chalkline
- Pencils
- Handsaw (Japanese saw)
- Keyhole saw

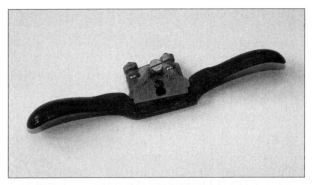

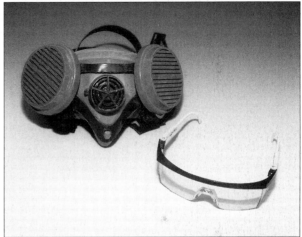

TOP: *A spokeshave is great for making paddles and cleaning up cockpit openings.* MIDDLE: *Safety glasses and a respirator: don't start work without them.* BOTTOM: *Pliers, a small hammer, side-cutters, a razor knife, and screwdrivers are some of the hand tools you'll need.*

- Drill and bits
- Block plane
- Screwdriver
- Clamps
- Pliers
- Rubber sanding block
- Side-cutters
- Small hammer
- Scissors
- Sawhorses

ADDITIONAL TOOLS FOR BUILDING FROM PLANS:

- Table saw (or access to one)
- Batten
- Architect's scale

MORE TOOLS YOU MAY WANT:

- More clamps
- Saber saw
- Electric sander
- Stapler
- Circular saw
- Spokeshave
- Chisels
- Mallet
- Marking gauge
- Engineer's scale
- Try square
- Bevel square
- Paint scraper
- Trammels

Setting Up Shop

You don't need a fancy shop to build a kayak. In fact, on nice days many builders move their work outside. What you do need is a space a few feet longer and at least 6 feet wider than the kayak you're building. Your garage, basement, attic, or shed will do if it has sufficient light, ventilation, and electrical power. Many woodworkers already have fully equipped shops that are too short for building a long kayak. If this is the case, make all the pieces in your shop, then assemble the kayak outside and move it into your hallway or living room at night.

Good light is essential when building a kayak; you must be able to judge curves, joints, and surface quality entirely by eye. And you must be certain that the almost colorless epoxy is evenly and completely spread over surfaces to be joined. If your shop isn't well lit, buy an inexpensive 48-inch fluorescent light fixture and hang it from the rafters or ceiling.

Building the kayaks featured in this book involves working with epoxy, varnish, paint, and acetone. In addition, you will produce copious quantities of sawdust. Breathing in these fumes and particles is both unhealthy and unpleasant. Your shop must have enough doors or windows for good ventilation. If it doesn't, or if you plan to build during the winter, install an exhaust fan. This can simply be a household fan set on a windowsill. In either case, use your respirator.

Professional power tools draw considerable amperage. If your shop's electrical power is supplied by an extension cord, be sure it's rated for the job. Extension cords used with power tools should be of at least 14-gauge wire (12-gauge is better); the longer the cord, the more crucial heavy wire is. Your tools will operate if you use a thin cord, but they will overheat and might burn out.

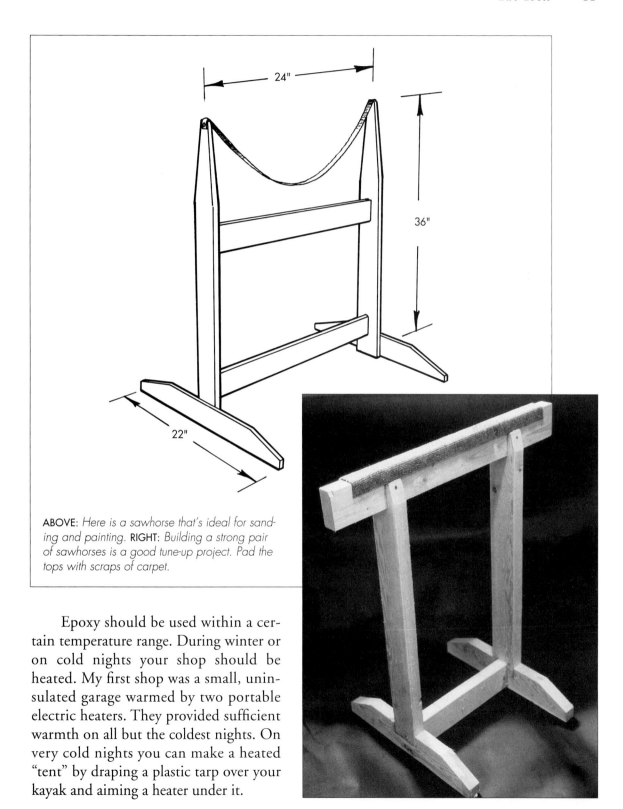

ABOVE: *Here is a sawhorse that's ideal for sanding and painting.* **RIGHT:** *Building a strong pair of sawhorses is a good tune-up project. Pad the tops with scraps of carpet.*

Epoxy should be used within a certain temperature range. During winter or on cold nights your shop should be heated. My first shop was a small, uninsulated garage warmed by two portable electric heaters. They provided sufficient warmth on all but the coldest nights. On very cold nights you can make a heated "tent" by draping a plastic tarp over your kayak and aiming a heater under it.

Equip your shop with a sturdy set of sawhorses to hold your kayak. Pad their tops with pieces of scrap carpet so your boat won't get scratched. You'll need a workbench or table on which to lay out your plans and to make and assemble smaller parts. Much of kayak building involves just sitting and thinking, so think about getting a stool or chair for your shop.

Supplies

Supplies you'll need for your shop:

- Sandpaper—80-, 220-, and 400-grit
- Disposable foam brushes with wooden, not plastic, handles
- Disposable bristle brushes, also called chip brushes
- Disposable foam rollers. These must be the short-nap yellow rollers that are also used for applying lacquer; never use the black-foam rollers.
- Epoxy-metering pumps or measuring cups
- Sticks for stirring (like Popsicle sticks)
- Disposable gloves (it's economical to buy them in a box of 100)

CHAPTER FOUR

The Materials

The resurgence of wooden boat building is due largely to the development of modern plywood and epoxy resins. The kayaks described in this book aren't really wooden boats in the traditional sense; they're more accurately described as wood-epoxy composites. Epoxy gives these boats many of the qualities associated with modern plastics—strength, durability, and resistance to corrosion and rot. Plywood frees the builder from the difficulties of finding long pieces of high-quality lumber and from dealing with the sometimes inconsistent strength of natural wood, yet it has wood's light weight, strength, and resiliency. And plywood can be worked with common and affordable tools.

The cost of the materials for building a kayak is small compared with the value of the time you'll devote to the project. Don't scrimp on materials—buy the best you can afford; the money you'll save by building your own boat will still be substantial. Good materials, like good tools, are more enjoyable to work with, and when your kayak is launched you won't worry about its integrity or its durability. If you can't afford good materials now, wait until you can; if you can't overcome the urge to use cheap materials, please do us both a favor and reconsider building your own boat.

Plywood

Plywood is manufactured from thin sheets of wood, called *veneers*, cut from tree trunks. These veneers are stacked and

TOP: *Plywood, whether thick or thin, should be stamped BS1088. BOTTOM: The top sheet of plywood has veneers in three different thicknesses; it's very stiff and definitely not suitable for compounded-plywood kayaks. The bottom sheet has a void; you can guess where this sheet would break if you tried to bend it. These are problems you'll avoid by using only BS1088 plywood.*

glued together to form a plywood panel; three to eleven layers of veneer make up a single sheet of plywood. The kayaks described in this book are built using 3 mm or 4 mm plywood made from three layers of veneer or 6 mm plywood made from five layers.

Stitch-and-glue boats should be built from marine-grade mahogany plywood. Any one of several types of mahogany plywood may be used, but *okoume*, a plantation-grown African mahogany, is the most economical and the most common. Other species such as *khaya* and *sapele* are also suitable, if a little heavier.

Mahogany plywood is not graded in the same manner as American exterior-grade plywood; it is made to various British standards. Look for wood stamped "BS1088," or British Standard 10.88. This is the proper grade for boatbuilding. BS1088 plywood is made in only a few mills in Europe, and is stocked by only twenty or thirty lumberyards in North America. Unless you live near a large city with a boatbuilding industry, you'll likely have to have the plywood shipped to you.

There is a surprising difference in quality even among BS1088 panels; in fact, I doubt that panels from some mills actually meet the standard. For this reason, you should only buy plywood from the most reputable distributors. Chesapeake Light Craft is one of the largest users of okoume plywood in the world, relying on several mills to meet its demand, so I've seen marine plywood from a wide variety of sources. Over the years, I've been most impressed by Shelman plywood, which is made by a Swiss-owned mill in Greece. Fortunately, Shelman has a huge mill, and its wood is relatively easy to find in many parts of the world.

You may also find plywood that's made to Lloyd's specifications, which usually also meets BS1088. Okoume plywood that's stamped BS6566 is exterior-grade plywood that may have very thin face veneers and may contain voids. It is not suitable for building hulls, but it can be used for some decks and interior components.

A few builders have built stitch-and-glue kayaks from *lauan*, or fir exterior-grade plywood. Unless the boat is specifically designed to be built from exterior-grade plywood, this is a potentially dangerous practice. Exterior-grade panels often contain voids that can cause them to crack suddenly. In addition, the exterior veneers, which are most important for strength, are often very thin. Exterior-grade panels also take much longer to finish than the better marine grades, so you lose in time what you saved in cost. Finally, consider that marine-grade plywood panels represent less than a third of the total cost of the materials used in most boats. If an inexpensive panel fails, you've wasted not only the plywood but also a lot of expensive fiberglass, epoxy, and other materials. Do not build the boats in this book from lauan plywood.

I'm often asked about using teak plywood for kayak construction. While teak is a lovely wood and probably the most durable of any species, it has limited applications in kayak building. What makes teak so durable is its high oil content; unfortunately, this oil makes teak difficult to glue. Teak is best left as solid wood for use as trim.

All domestic marine-grade plywood is made from Douglas fir. Douglas fir is a superb solid wood—light, strong, and durable. Unfortunately, it makes poor plywood for kayak hulls. Because Douglas fir grows in temperate regions, its growth rate varies from season to season; thus, it has different rates of expansion and contraction. This means that Douglas fir plywood is prone to *checking*, or splitting. Additionally, the nature of fir and the quality standards of American plywood manufacturers combine to make this plywood unattractive and difficult to finish. Fir plywood can be used for coaming spacers, bulkheads, and other parts where bending properties and appearance aren't important, though for these applications exterior-grade plywood is sufficient.

Solid Wood

Though the hulls of the kayaks in this book are of plywood, many of the internal parts are made from solid wood. Most of the solid wood used in a kayak will be ripped into thin strips for *sheer clamps* (stringers running along the top of the hull panels), hatch beams, and other small parts. So you won't need the large high-quality boards used in traditional boat-building. Short pieces of wood can easily be joined with scarf joints to make up the few longer bits you'll need. All the wood in a kayak is protected by layers of epoxy and varnish or paint. Since wooden kayaks are not left in the water for long periods of time (as are large motorboats and sail-boats) and are stored under cover, you need not be overly concerned about the durability of the solid woods you choose.

Spruce, whether Sitka spruce or east-ern spruce, is a good choice for parts that must be strong, stiff, and light, such as sheer clamps. Sitka spruce has long been prized for sailboat masts and airplane parts because it's available in long, *clear* (knot-free) lengths. Today, however, it's expensive and difficult to find. Eastern spruce, though not usually clear, is readily found in most lumberyards as dimensional lumber used for home building. If you take the time to sort through a pile of good-quality eastern spruce, you'll find enough clear pieces to build a kayak and pay far less than you would have for Sitka spruce. It's most economical to buy eastern spruce in 1-inch by 4-inch by 16-foot lengths and then rip it to width. It may be hard to find 16-foot lengths that are en-tirely free of knots, but they're cheap enough that you can simply discard strips that contain more than one tight knot.

Cypress is a strong, light, rot-resistant wood that is often available in long, clear lengths. It is a traditional boatbuilding wood in the southeastern United States. At Chesapeake Light Craft cypress is the pre-ferred material for sheer clamps in kayak kits.

Douglas fir, or Oregon pine, is an-other good choice. It's a little heavier than spruce, but somewhat stronger. Douglas fir is easy to find at lumberyards, where long, clear boards are common, and it's inexpen-sive. The grain of Douglas fir varies con-siderably, so look through a pile to find the best pieces; try to select boards that are light in weight and have a straight grain. The main disadvantage of Douglas fir is its brittleness. It has a tendency to crack when bent, and it may check if it is left ex-posed to the weather.

Cedar is another wood sometimes used in kayaks. There are several varieties of cedar. Alaska cedar, Port Orford cedar, and white cedar are light, soft woods suitable for sheer clamps, *carlins* (fore-and-aft deck beams), and other parts. Cedar isn't quite as strong as spruce or fir however, so the parts should be made a little thicker. Western red cedar is the only species of cedar that should be avoided; it's simply not strong enough for some structural uses.

Like many woodworkers, you may have a cache of mahogany, ash, clear pine, or other cabinet-grade lumber. There's no reason not to use these woods in your kayak, except that it may increase its weight and cost slightly. I like to add a few trim pieces of exotic wood to enhance the appearance of a boat.

Epoxy

Marine epoxy adhesives must be used in stitch-and-glue boatbuilding. Other resins and glues, such as polyester or vinylester, simply aren't strong enough to hold the panels together. And none are as versatile: you'll use epoxy as a glue, as an adhesive coating when applying fiberglass tape and cloth, as a sealant to protect and waterproof bare wood, and as a gap filler and fairing compound. Several companies market extensive epoxy systems consisting of various resins, hardeners, thickening additives, and application tools. I've had particularly good results with MAS and West System brands.

Epoxy consists of two parts: the *resin* and a *hardener*; the hardener is mixed with the resin to make it *cure*, or set. Since the ratio of resin to hardener varies among brands of epoxy, it's critical that you mix the two precisely to the manufacturer's instructions. Epoxy that has too much or too little hardener will not achieve full strength when cured, or it may not cure at all.

Since epoxy resin and hardener are thick and sticky, using cups to measure them is both inaccurate and unpleasant. Most epoxy manufacturers sell inexpensive *calibrated metering pumps* for this purpose. These plastic pumps screw into the tops of the resin and hardener con-

The epoxy table—everything needed is at hand. Notice the epoxy-metering pumps and the various thickeners; this should excite you closet chemists out there.

tainers and precisely meter the liquids. You simply pump one stroke of resin for one stroke of hardener; the epoxy and hardener are automatically dispensed at the exact ratio required, and you only need to stir them thoroughly. Increasing the amount of hardener will not result in a faster cure, but it will result in a much weaker epoxy.

Epoxy is thinner than most glues and will flow out of gaps and joints unless it's first mixed with a *thickening agent*, or *filler*. Epoxy manufacturers sell many types of thickening agents. A good choice for gluing is *silica powder* or *silica fibers*. *Wood*

flour and *chopped fibers* are used for making fillets and filling gaps. Microballoons and Microlight make lightweight, easily sanded fillers for fairing and for fillets in racing boats. Thickeners do not have any chemical effect on the mix; they simply make the epoxy thicker. Never confuse hardener and thickener: a hardener is always mixed into the resin to make it cure, whereas a thickener is sometimes added to the epoxy for specific applications.

The amount and type of thickener added to the epoxy varies with the application. Here are four "recipes" that will cover any epoxy use in kayak building:

Four epoxy "recipes" for kayak building: (1) clear epoxy, for coating; (2) epoxy mixed with silica powder for gluing wood-to-wood joints; (3) a thick mixture of epoxy and wood flour used in fillets and for filling gaps; (4) a mixture of epoxy and microballoons for fairing.

- When coating, sealing, or saturating wood with epoxy, don't add any thickening powder.
- To use epoxy as a glue to join wood to wood, add enough silica powder to the mix of resin and hardener to bring it to the consistency of mayonnaise or jam. Let the mix sit on the joint for a minute or two before clamping.
- To fill gaps or make a fillet, add sufficient filler, such as wood flour, to make a peanut butter–like paste.
- To fair a rough surface or fill a nonstructural gap, mix in microballoons or other lightweight, easily sanded filler to make a putty.

It is critical to mix the resin and the hardener thoroughly before adding a thickener and then mix again. One epoxy manufacturer estimates that 90 percent of epoxy problems are caused by improper mixing.

Since epoxy is readily absorbed by wood, it will affect the wood's bending properties. For this reason, it's important to wipe up any epoxy that oozes out of joints before it can harden. It's also important not to "starve" the joints. If too little epoxy is used, it will all be absorbed by the wood, leaving a joint that is dry and weak. Likewise, if a joint is to be clamped, let the epoxy sit on the wood for a few minutes to determine whether more is needed before joining the parts permanently. Don't apply any more clamping pressure than is needed to make a tight joint or you'll squeeze all the epoxy out.

Cured epoxy must be sanded lightly before another layer of epoxy may be applied. Also check for *amine blush*, a waxy film that can form on the surface of cured epoxy; it must be removed with soapy water and a scrub pad before overcoating to obtain a strong secondary bond. MAS epoxy, if used with its slow hardener, does not usually blush, which is one reason that I use that brand. If you overcoat epoxy within about forty-eight hours of the initial application, no surface preparation should be required.

The rate at which epoxy cures is greatly affected by the ambient temperature, so epoxy manufacturers offer *fast* and *slow* hardeners. Epoxy catalyzed by a slow hardener will remain workable longer in warm weather, which is often desirable. On the other hand, resin mixed with a slow hardener will not reliably cure in less than twenty-four hours unless the temperature is over 70°F. A fast hardener will cure more quickly, and at cooler temperatures (the minimum working temperature for most epoxies is around 60°F). MAS also offers a "Cool Cure" resin and hardener specifically for use in unheated or underheated shops.

As the epoxy cures it generates heat, which accelerates the cure time. A large batch of epoxy mixed in a deep cup will heat up and harden very rapidly, often in a matter of minutes. When the same amount of epoxy is quickly spread out however, such as when coating a boat's hull, it may take hours to harden. In the first instance there is relatively little surface area, so the heat generated is not dissipated and the epoxy solidifies rapidly. Conversely, the thin film of epoxy has a much larger surface area, which allows the heat to dissipate.

Epoxy Safety

Epoxy resins, hardeners, and solvents contain potentially dangerous chemicals. Always read the warnings from the epoxy or solvent manufacturer, and follow these simple safety rules:

- Avoid getting epoxy on your skin; wear disposable gloves and be neat when you work. Continual contact with epoxy can lead to sensitization: you may develop an allergy to epoxy and never be able to work with it again.
- Clean tools and spills with acetone or lacquer thinner, but don't use them to remove epoxy from your skin. Solvents can actually drive the chemical into your skin. Instead, use soap and water, vinegar, or, best of all, waterless hand cleaners such as those used by auto mechanics.
- Unlike polyester or vinylester resins, epoxy has little odor, but you should still wear a respirator when sanding it.
- Avoid breathing dust from thickening powders, particularly silica-based powders, which are essentially powdered glass.
- While epoxy is not particularly flammable, acetone and other solvents used for cleanup are very volatile: Keep them away from open flames and space heaters.
- Always read the epoxy container and other literature provided by the manufacturer.

When long working times are important, always get the epoxy out of the mixing container quickly. A useful technique is to pour the epoxy into a shallow bowl or pie tin to increase the working time. Since containers of curing epoxy can generate a significant amount of heat, always place extra mixed epoxy outdoors.

In addition to the dispensing pumps and disposable mixing cups such as paper drink cups, yogurt containers, or clean tin cans, a few inexpensive accessories and supplies make using epoxy systems much easier. You should have sticks for stirring, as well as disposable brushes, foam rollers, and a plastic squeegee or plastic putty knife for applying the epoxy. A soupspoon makes a good tool for applying fillets. When coating large, flat areas, use a no-lint foam roller: cut a full-width roller cover in half and use it on a 3-inch roller frame.

One last tip about working with epoxy: this stuff is unbelievably gooey and sticky, and once it hardens it's impossible to remove from clothes, carpet, and furniture. "Work clean," as we say in boatbuilding shops.

Fasteners

Very few metal fasteners are needed in a plywood kayak. In fact, you could build one of these boats with no metal at all. Most kayaks, however, will contain a few screws, ring nails, and some copper wire.

I prefer to use silicon-bronze fasteners whenever possible. Available only from marine suppliers, these are expensive, but you won't need many. Some builders prefer stainless steel, but you should know that stainless steel comes in various grades, some of which are not very stainless at all. So, particularly if you'll be paddling in salt water, buy your screws from a reputable marine dealer. Don't substitute brass or copper fasteners for bronze: they are not nearly as strong nor as corrosion-resistant. And please don't try to save a few cents by using ordinary steel or galvanized fasteners—wouldn't you feel silly if you had big rust streaks down the side of your kayak? If you use staples, use stainless steel, Monel, or bronze staples in case one breaks off in the wood or you forget to remove one.

The other metal fastener you will use is uninsulated copper wire for stitching the hull together. I prefer 18-gauge wire, which used to be sold at hardware stores for hanging birdfeeders and tying up roses. Today, bare copper wire can be hard to find; you may have to order it from a marine or boatbuilder's supply house. Copper wire is best because it's easy to cut and to sand flush with the wood. Stainless steel wire is available, but it's very stiff, hard to twist, and very difficult to sand. Another

Here are all the bronze fasteners, ring nails, and screws that go into a kayak. Don't be a cheapskate and substitute brass or galvanized hardware.

option is the plastic ties used to secure electrical wiring, which are inexpensive and available at any electronics or electrical supply house. The smallest size will pass through a ⅛-inch hole; that's bigger than a hole for copper wire, but if the boat is to be painted, it hardly matters. A few builders use heavy monofilament fishing line instead because it's almost invisible—but imagine tying all those knots.

Finding Materials

Asking for okoume plywood at most lumberyards will result in little more than a funny look from the salesperson. Marine

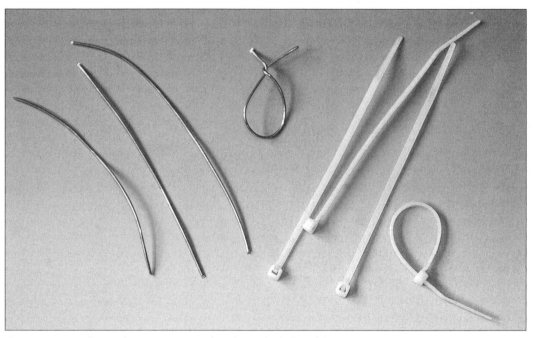

Copper wire or electrical wire ties are used to clamp the hull until the epoxy sets.

plywood, epoxies, and fasteners are specialty items. If you don't live in a traditional boatbuilding area, you'll probably have to order at least some of your materials by mail. Ask local boatbuilders where they buy materials or look through the ads in *WoodenBoat* magazine for local sources. Suppliers who sell by mail are listed in the Resource Appendix beginning on page 185.

CHAPTER FIVE

The Plans

The New Kayak Shop contains plans for three new designs. Two of these, the Chesapeake 16 and the West River 180, are recent designs that might have been called state-of-the-art in 1999. The third design, the Severn, is one of my older designs; it's built using the compounded-plywood method of construction.

I chose the plans for these three kayaks to illustrate three methods of kayak construction. You'll be able to judge from my descriptions whether one of them is the sort of boat you want. If, however, you require a kayak that's not drawn here, then go out and find or draw the plans for it. Never choose a kayak design simply because the plans for it are in front of you. And please don't build the wrong boat

simply to save a few dollars on plans. In fact, I will state right at the outset, and in no uncertain terms, that building a boat using only the plans in a book or magazine, including this book, is foolish. Yes, I know that many builders have done just that; I've even built boats from plans in magazines. But in most cases they and I would have saved time and money by buying the full-size set of plans.

There are several good reasons to buy a full-size set of plans. Purchasing the plans entitles you to technical help from the designer or his or her staff. Most designers won't help you build a boat if you have not purchased plans—they could never make a living if they did. Plans purchased from the designer will contain the

The Chesapeake 16 is the easiest boat in this book to build.

latest revisions; builders often call the designer with new ideas and to point out errors on plans. On two occasions I've sent letters to customers when I transposed numbers on the first run of a new set of plans. Having a fresh set of plans will result in a better boat. There will be full-scale patterns for many of the parts, which will greatly reduce the amount of time spent laying them out. And finally, though I am fortunate that Chesapeake Light Craft has been a commercial success, this is uncommon in the boat design business. It has allowed me to publish plans in books and magazine with little regard to payment, but most boat designers practice their craft with limited financial reward; they simply love boats. Those of us who build their craft owe them something for their designs. Think of yourself as a patron of the art of kayak design.

Nevertheless, the plans in this book are complete and contain all the information required to build these kayaks. Should you choose to build only from the plans in this book, you can scale up some patterns and redraw most of the parts to full size. With the aid of an engineer's scale, a tape measure, and a calculator this is not difficult; however, these plans are reduced from full size to fit on these pages, and lose some clarity and detail in the process. Of course, dimensions are given for all of the critical hull parts and bulkheads.

Deciphering boat plans can be frustrating for novice builders and, for that matter, for experienced builders. I spent many years sitting in my office at a civil-engineering firm answering questions from contractors, developers, and county inspectors who couldn't understand something in our plans. This was quite frustrating since those plans seemed, to me, simple as could be. Eventually it drove me to building kayaks. I finally realized that most draftsmen and designers really do strive to make their plans easy to understand, but what's obvious to one person is often obtuse to another. Having a good, clean set of full-size drawings, the accompanying instructions, and a little patience will allow you to answer most questions. A call or note to the designer will answer the rest.

The Chesapeake 16

I drew the hard-chine Chesapeake sea kayak as a replacement for the Cape Charles model featured in *The Kayak Shop*. This newer model is easier to build, faster, stronger, roomier, and more seaworthy. It also handles better in rough seas and strong beam winds.

This combination of good handling, speed, solid tracking, and large volume have made this model remarkably popular—Chesapeake Light Craft sells thousands of precut kits for the Chesapeake kayak each year. The model has been praised in numerous magazine reviews and chosen for several expeditions. I have also drawn a 17-foot and an 18-foot version of this model. In addition, there are three lower-volume versions of this boat, the Chesapeake LT 16, LT 17, and LT 18, for folks who don't need to carry a lot of camping gear. "LT" stands for "light touring". The Chesapeake 16 is actually 15 feet, 9 inches long, with a 23½-inch beam and a weight of about 42 pounds. It's the easiest of the Chesapeakes, and of the boats in this book, to build.

The Chesapeake 16 makes a great touring kayak for paddlers weighing up to about 180 pounds; the total burden is about 240 pounds. Heavier paddlers or those who need to carry more gear should build one of the larger versions: the Chesapeake 17 is designed for paddlers weighing 160 to 220 pounds, and the 18-footer is for paddlers over 200 pounds. The larger boats are not simply scaled-up versions of the Chesapeake 16; though they share many characteristics, they are different designs.

If you seek a general-purpose touring boat capable of carrying a substantial load of camping gear, I can think of no

(continued on page 60)

The Chesapeake is easy to paddle in calm creeks or in open water.

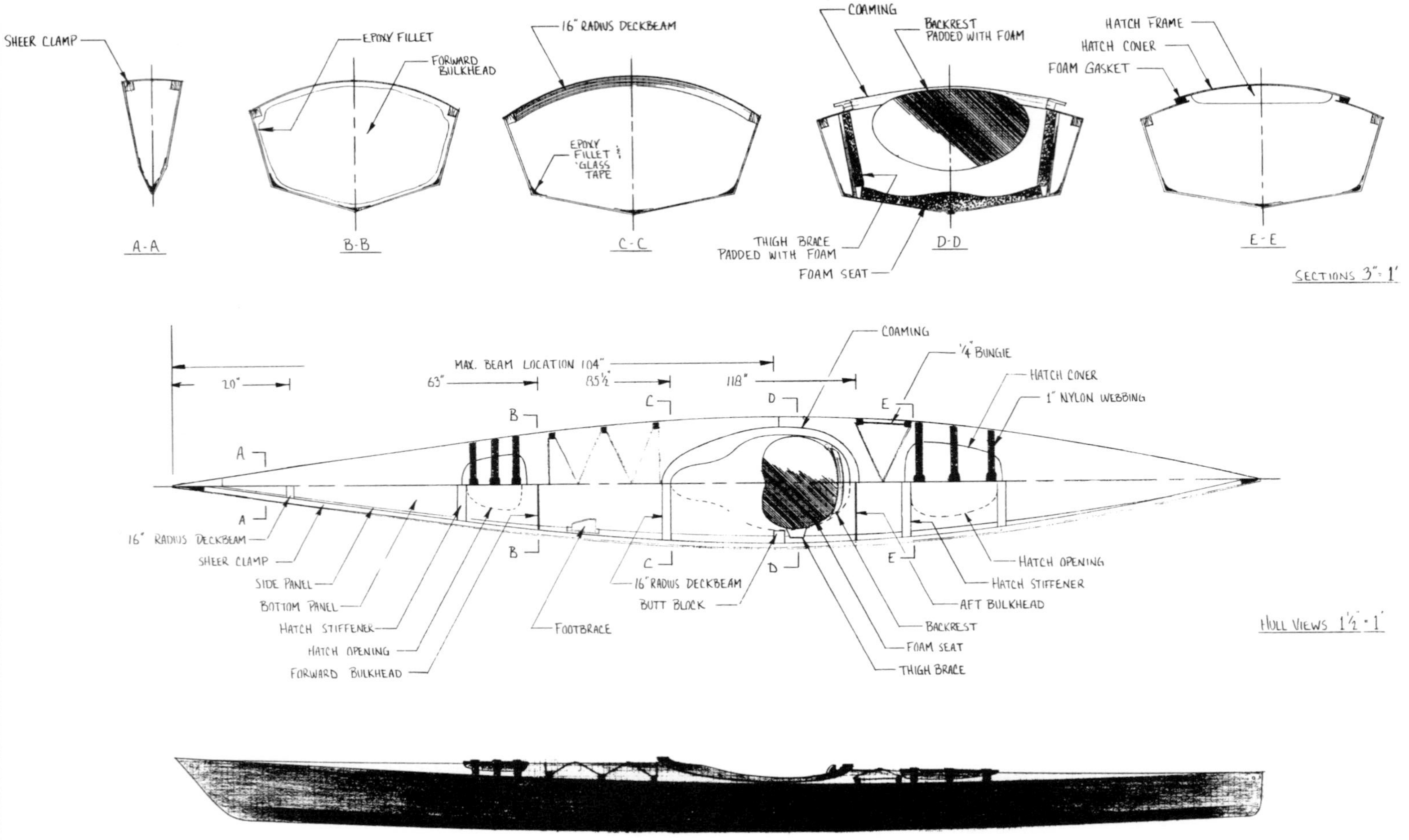

SHEET 1

SECTIONS 3" = 1'

HULL VIEWS 1½" = 1'

A-A

SHEER CLAMP

B-B

FORWARD BULKHEAD

EPOXY FILLET

C-C

16" RADIUS DECKBEAM

EPOXY FILLET ¾" GLASS TAPE

D-D

COAMING

BACKREST PADDED WITH FOAM

THIGH BRACE PADDED WITH FOAM

FOAM SEAT

E-E

HATCH FRAME

HATCH COVER

FOAM GASKET

MAX. BEAM LOCATION 104"

118"

85½"

63"

10"

COAMING

¼" BUNGIE

HATCH COVER

1" NYLON WEBBING

HATCH OPENING

HATCH STIFFENER

AFT BULKHEAD

BACKREST

FOAM SEAT

THIGH BRACE

16" RADIUS DECKBEAM

BUTT BLOCK

FOOTBRACE

SIDE PANEL

BOTTOM PANEL

HATCH STIFFENER

HATCH OPENING

FORWARD BULKHEAD

THIGH BRACE

16" RADIUS DECKBEAM

SHEER CLAMP

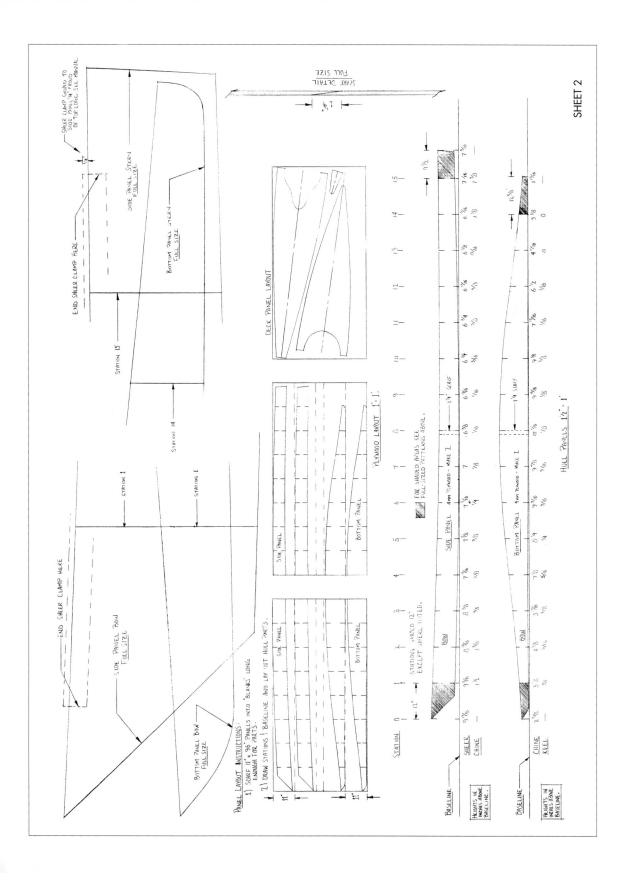

SHEET 2

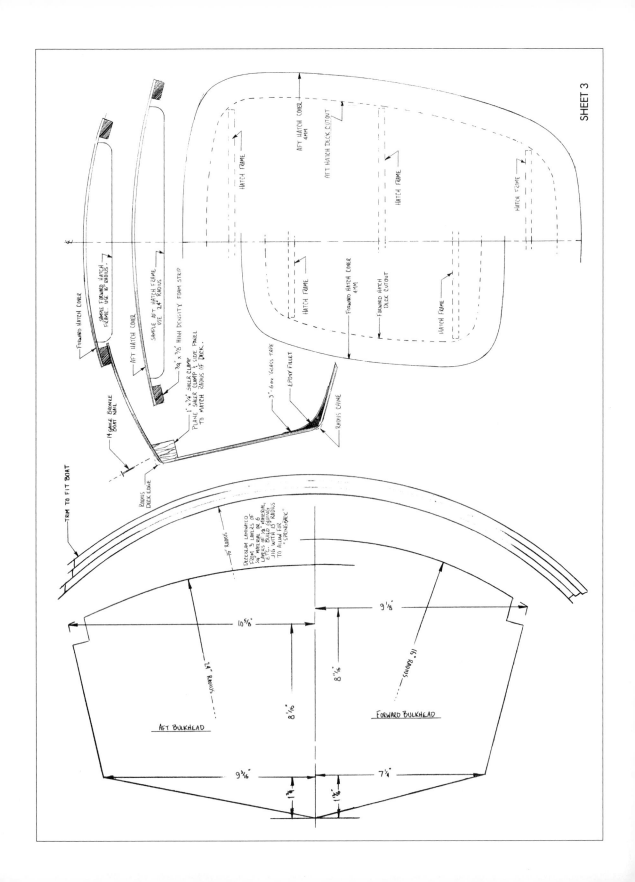

SHEET 3

Forward Hatch Cover

Sample Forward Hatch Frame. Use 16" Radius.

Aft Hatch Cover

Sample Aft Hatch Frame. Use 24" Radius

3/4" x 3/8" High Density Foam Strip

1" x 3/4" Sheer Clamp. Plane Sheer Clamp & Side Panel to Match Radius of Deck.

3"- 6oz Glass Tape

Epoxy Fillet

Radius Chine

14 Gauge Bronze Boat Nail

Trim to Fit Boat

Radius Deck Edge

Hatch Frame

Aft Hatch Cover 4mm

Aft Hatch Deck Cutout

Hatch Frame

Hatch Frame

Hatch Frame

Forward Hatch Cover 4mm

Forward Hatch Deck Cutout

Hatch Frame

Hatch Frame

16" Radius

Decoglam Laminated From 3 Layers of 3/4 Material or 6 Layers of 3/8 Material, etc. Build Gluing Jig With 15" Radius to Allow for "Springback"

Aft Bulkhead

Forward Bulkhead

10 5/8"

9 1/8"

14" Radius

16" Radius

8 1/16"

8 1/16"

9 3/16"

7 1/4"

1"

1 1/4"

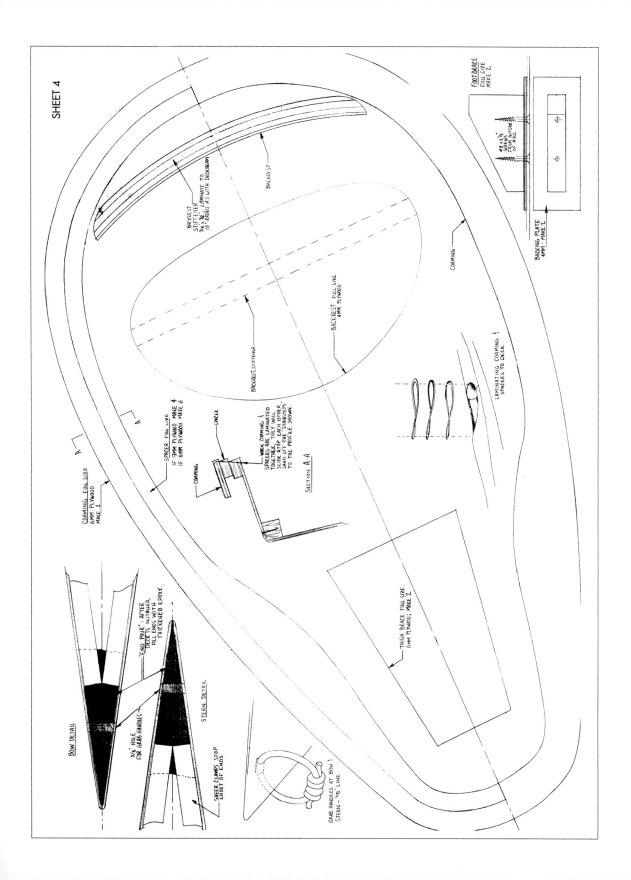

FOOTBRACE
FULL SIZE
MAKE 2

#6 × 1½
SCREWS
FROM OUTSIDE
OF HULL

BACKING PLATE
4MM · MAKE 2

BACKREST

BACKREST
STIFFENER
¾ × ¾; LAMINATE TO
16" RADIUS AS WITH DECKBEAMS

BACKREST, STIFFENER

BACKREST FULL SIZE
4MM PLYWOOD

COMING

SPACER FULL SIZE
IF 9MM PLYWOOD MAKE 4
IF 6MM PLYWOOD MAKE 6

SPACER

COMING

WHEN COMING &
SPACERS ARE LAMINATED
TOGETHER, THEY WILL
SLIDE ATOP EACH OTHER,
SAND OFF THE 'STAIRSTEPS'
TO THE PROFILE SHOWN.

SECTION A·A

LAMINATING COMING &
SPACERS TO DECK.

COMING FULL SIZE
6MM PLYWOOD
MAKE 1

THIGH BRACE FULL SIZE.
6MM PLYWOOD; MAKE 2

BOW DETAIL

"END POUR": AFTER
DECKS IS INSTALLED,
FILL ENDS WITH
THICKENED EPOXY.

¾" HOLE
FOR GRAB HANDLES

STERN DETAIL

SHEER CLAMPS STOP
SHORT OF ENDS

GRAB HANDLES AT BOW &
STERN - ⅜ LINE

(continued from page 55) design I would recommend over the Chesapeake. For the novice paddler, this is a boat you won't outgrow. In the hands of a skilled paddler, the Chesapeake is capable of long coastal trips.

CHESAPEAKE 16
BILL OF MATERIALS

- 3 sheets 4 mm BS1088 okoume marine plywood
- ½ sheet 6 mm BS1088 okoume marine plywood
- 32 feet of 1- by ¾-inch spruce, fir, or other strong, light wood
- 2 gallons catalyzed marine epoxy
- thickening agents for epoxy (silica, wood flour)
- 50-yard roll of 3-inch, 6- or 9-ounce fiberglass tape
- 8 yards of 6-ounce, 38-inch-wide fiberglass cloth
- 50 feet of 18-gauge bare copper wire
- 30 #10 1-inch bronze screws and finish washers
- 4 #8 1½-inch bronze wood screws
- 4 ounces of ¾-inch, 14- or 15-gauge bronze ring nails
- 24- by 24-inch sheet ¾-inch Minicel foam
- 8 feet of 1-inch high-density foam weather stripping
- 6 1-inch plastic Fastex buckles
- 18 feet of 1-inch nylon webbing
- 2 board feet of pine, spruce, or similar wood
- kayak backband and hardware (optional)
- 9 feet of 1-inch nylon webbing (if

installing plywood and foam seatback)
- 2 cam buckles (if installing plywood and foam seatback)
- 1 ladderlock (tension lock) buckle (if installing plywood and foam seatback)
- footbraces

The West River 180

I designed the West River 180 as a very fast and rugged multi-chine kayak for the experienced paddler. The hull is based on my earlier West River 162 and 164 designs, which have proven popular with paddlers. The West River 180's waterline length is almost 17½ feet so that it will provide enough speed when we're feeling strong. The prismatic coefficient is 0.55, moderately high, to take full advantage of this long waterline. A beam of 22 inches in a hull with firm bilges provides reasonable initial stability while still retaining a fairly low wetted-surface area. The kayak's dimensions, 18 feet by 22 inches, are the maximum length and minimum beam allowed in the "touring class" in many sea kayak races. It has a low but buoyant bow, some flare for good secondary stability, and moderate rocker. Since it is a touring boat, it has 11½ inches of depth—my size 11½ feet in rubber boots will fit with room to spare.

The West River 180's multi-chine hull has many more parts than the Chesapeake's hard-chine hull, so it takes longer to lay out and build. Most multi-chine, stitch-and-glue kayaks are built from precut kits. But armed with a good design and attention to

The West River is a fast touring kayak for the experienced paddler.

detail, even a first-time builder can complete a multi-chine kayak from plans. Building the West River doesn't require complicated joinery or tricky carpentry, but it does require great care in laying out and cutting the panels. They must be shaped very accurately and joined carefully, and the epoxy and fiberglass work must be neat.

The West River is faster and more efficient than the Chesapeake but has less initial and secondary stability, is less maneuverable, and is more challenging to build.

WEST RIVER BILL OF MATERIALS

- 4 sheets 4 mm BS1088 okoume marine plywood
- ½ sheet 6 mm BS1088 okoume marine plywood
- 36 feet of ¾- by 1-inch spruce, fir, or other strong, light wood
- 2 gallons catalyzed marine epoxy
- thickening agents for epoxy (silica, wood flour)
- 12 yards of 6-ounce, 38-inch-wide fiberglass cloth
- 100 feet of 18-gauge bare copper wire
- 27 #10 1-inch bronze screws and finish washers
- 2 #8 1½-inch bronze wood screws
- 4 ounces of ¾-inch, 14-gauge bronze ring shank nails
- 24 feet of shock cord
- 24- by 24-inch sheet ¾-inch Minicel foam
- 8 feet of 1- by ⅜-inch high-density foam weather stripping
- 6 1-inch plastic side-release buckles
- 18 feet of 1-inch flat nylon webbing
- backband
- footbraces

(continued on page 67)

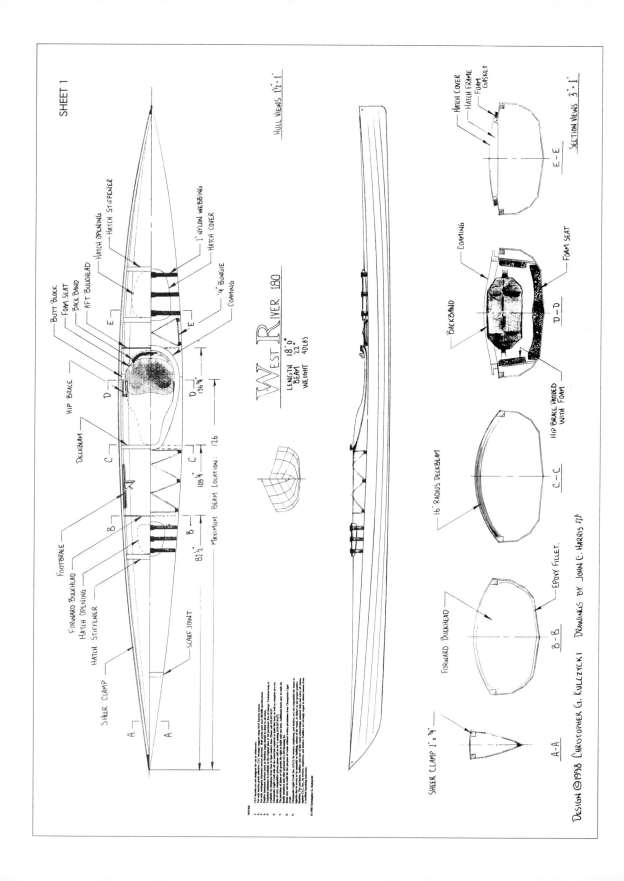

SHEET 1

HULL VIEWS 1½" · 1'

SHEER CLAMP

HATCH STIFFENER
HATCH OPENING
FORWARD BULKHEAD
FOOTBRACE
DECKBEAM
HIP BRACE

BUTT BLOCK
FOAM SEAT
BACK BAND
AFT BULKHEAD
HATCH OPENING
HATCH STIFFENER

1" NYLON WEBBING
HATCH COVER
¼" BUNGIE
COAMING

SCARF JOINT

MAXIMUM BEAM LOCATION : 126

82½"   105¼"   136¾"

WEST RIVER 180

LENGTH   18' 0"
BEAM   22"
WEIGHT   40 LBS

HATCH COVER
HATCH FRAME
FOAM
GASKET

E–E

COAMING
BACKBAND
FOAM SEAT

HIP BRACE PADDED
WITH FOAM

D–D

16" RADIUS DECKBEAM

C–C

SECTION VIEWS 3" · 1'

FORWARD BULKHEAD

EPOXY FILLET.

B–B

SHEER CLAMP 1" × ¾"

A–A

DESIGN ©1998 CHRISTOPHER G. KULCZYCKI   DRAWINGS BY JOHN C. HARRIS JR.

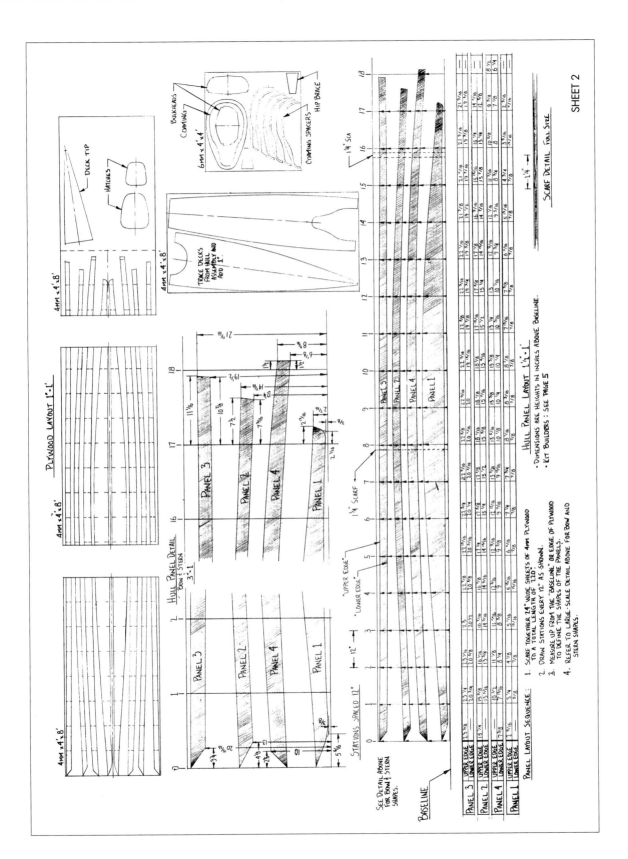

SHEET 2

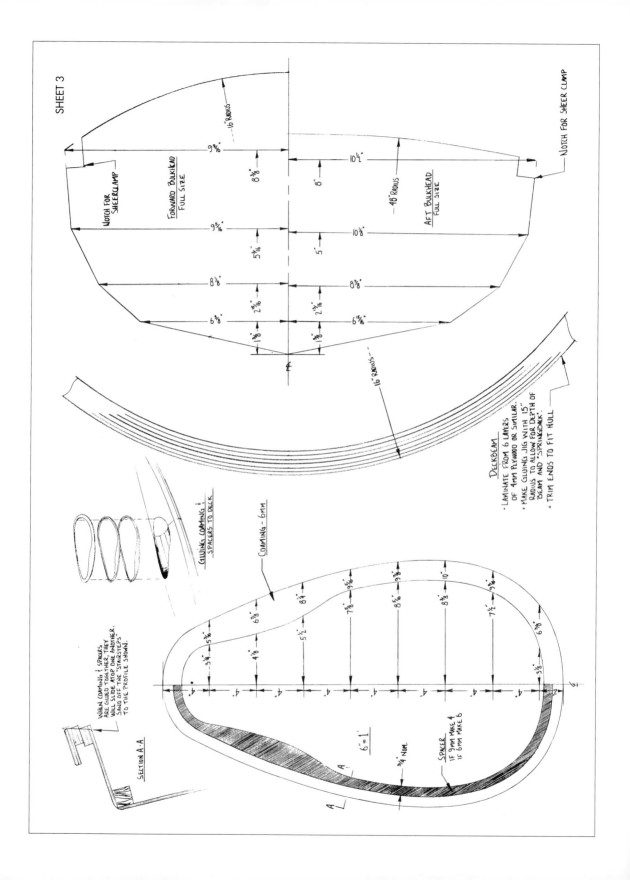

SHEET 3

NOTCH FOR SHEER CLAMP

16" RADIUS

9⁹⁄₁₆"

8³⁄₈"

FORWARD BULKHEAD
FULL SIZE

NOTCH FOR
SHEER CLAMP

9⁵⁄₁₆"

5⁵⁄₁₆"

8¹⁄₈"

2⁵⁄₁₆"

6³⁄₈"

1³⁄₈"

₵

10½"

8"

48" RADIUS

AFT BULKHEAD
FULL SIZE

NOTCH FOR SHEER CLAMP

10⅛"

5"

8⅞"

2³⁄₁₆"

6¹⁵⁄₁₆"

⅞"

16" RADIUS

DECKBEAM
• LAMINATE FROM 6 LAYERS
  OF 4MM PLYWOOD OR SIMILAR.
• MAKE GLUING JIG WITH 15"
  RADIUS TO ALLOW FOR DEPTH OF
  BEAM AND "SPRINGBACK".
• TRIM ENDS TO FIT HULL.

GLUING COMING:
SPACERS TO DECK

COAMING - 6MM

WHEN COAMING & SPACERS
ARE GLUED TOGETHER, THEY
WILL SLIDE ATOP ONE ANOTHER.
SAND OFF THE "STAIRSTEPS"
TO THE PROFILE SHOWN.

SECTION A-A

3¼"

5⁵⁄₁₆"

6⅝"

8¼"

4⅛"

5½"

7⅞"

9⁵⁄₁₆"

8⁵⁄₁₆"

9⅞"

10"

8⅜"

7½"

9¾"

3⅜"

6⁷⁄₁₆"

6" = 1'

¾" NOM.

SPACER
IF 9MM MAKE 4
IF 6MM MAKE 6

A

A

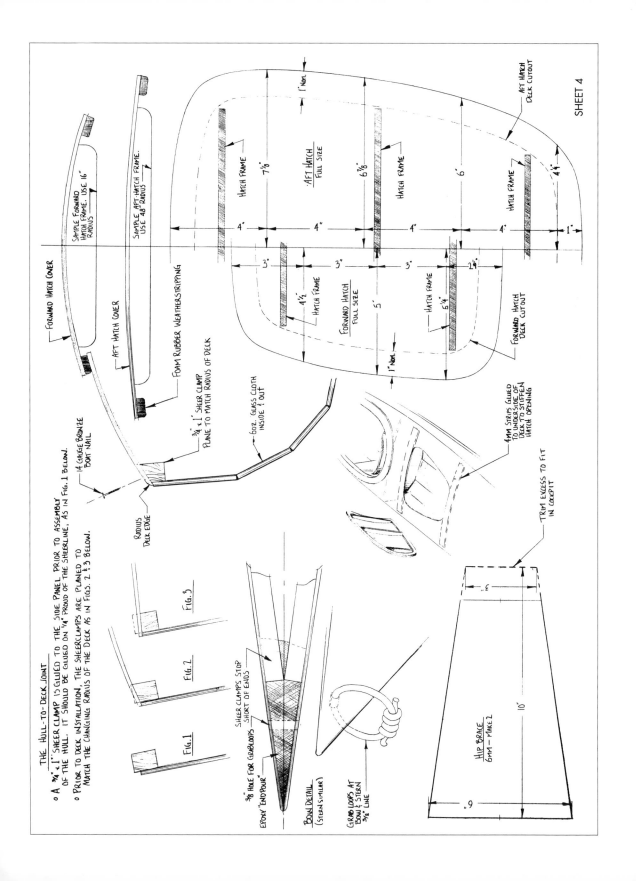

THE HULL-TO-DECK JOINT

o A 3/4" x 1" SHEER CLAMP IS GLUED TO THE SIDE PANEL PRIOR TO ASSEMBLY OF THE HULL. IT SHOULD BE GLUED ON 1/4" PROUD OF THE SHEERLINE, AS IN FIG. 1 BELOW.

o PRIOR TO DECK INSTALLATION, THE SHEERCLAMPS ARE PLANED TO MATCH THE CHANGING RADIUS OF THE DECK AS IN FIGS. 2 & 3 BELOW.

SHEET 4

FORWARD HATCH COVER

SAMPLE FORWARD HATCH FRAME. USE 16" RADIUS

SAMPLE AFT HATCH FRAME. USE 48" RADIUS

AFT HATCH COVER

FOAM RUBBER WEATHERSTRIPPING

3/4" x 1" SHEER CLAMP PLANE TO MATCH RADIUS OF DECK

14 GAUGE BRONZE BOAT NAIL

RADIUS DECK EDGE

6 OZ. GLASS CLOTH INSIDE & OUT

1" NOM.

HATCH FRAME

7 1/8"

AFT HATCH
FULL SIZE

AFT HATCH DECK CUTOUT

4" 4"

HATCH FRAME

6 7/8"

6"

HATCH FRAME

4" 4" 1"

4 4"

3" 3" 3" 2 4"

4 1/2"
HATCH FRAME

FORWARD HATCH
FULL SIZE

5"

HATCH FRAME

5 1/4"

FORWARD HATCH DECK CUTOUT

1" NOM.

4MM STRIPS GLUED TO UNDERSIDE OF DECK TO STIFFEN HATCH OPENING

TRIM EXCESS TO FIT IN COCKPIT

FIG. 3

FIG. 2

FIG. 1

SHEER CLAMPS STOP SHORT OF ENDS

3/8 HOLE FOR GRABLOOPS

EPOXY "ENDPOUR"

BOW DETAIL
(STERN SIMILAR)

GRAB LOOPS AT BOW & STERN 3/8" LINE

3"

10"

HIP BRACE
6MM – MAKE 2

9"

6"

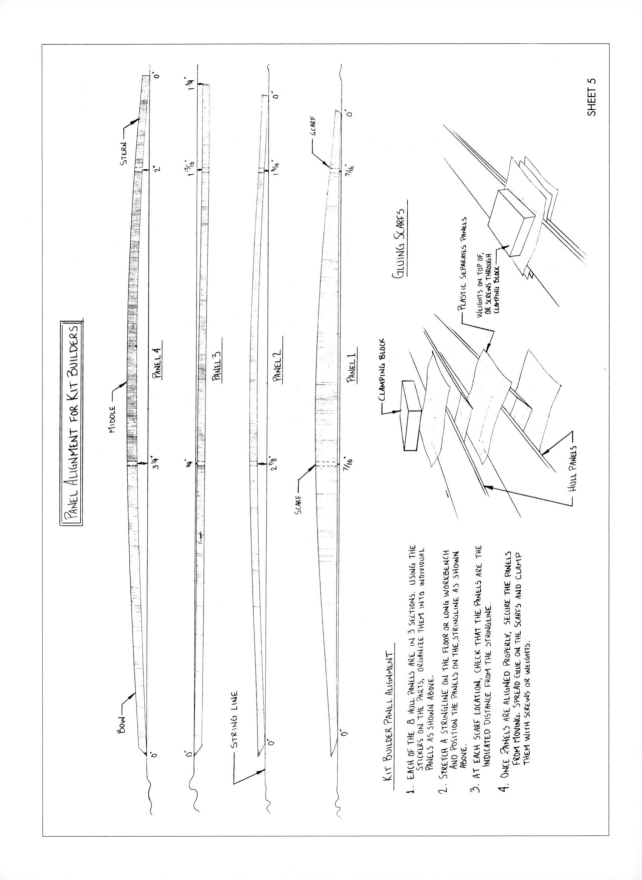

Strong paddlers will appreciate the West River's speed potential.

(continued from page 61)

The Severn

The Severn is a small, ultralight flatwater kayak. It measures 14 feet, 7 inches by 25 inches and weighs 26 pounds. It's best suited for paddlers weighing less than 180 pounds who are not too tall and have no wish to carry camping gear. It tracks well and can handle a fair chop, though I would certainly not classify it as a sea kayak. Its light weight and amazing efficiency make this kayak special. Even a child can get it off a car's roof rack, shoulder it, and walk some distance to the water's edge. And once launched, it displays reassuring stability and requires almost no effort to paddle. Because of its short waterline, this kayak's top speed is not high, but it will glide along all day at a moderate pace without tiring the paddler. And for many, that is far more important than speed.

The Severn is, however, a fast boat to build, although—as with all compounded-plywood craft—the process is tricky and not at all intuitive. Of the three kayaks in this book, it is the hardest to make. The hull and deck are constructed from 3 mm plywood, so the Severn is not as rugged as the Chesapeake and the West River, which are built from 4 mm plywood. The Severn must be built from top-quality 3 mm

(continued on page 71)

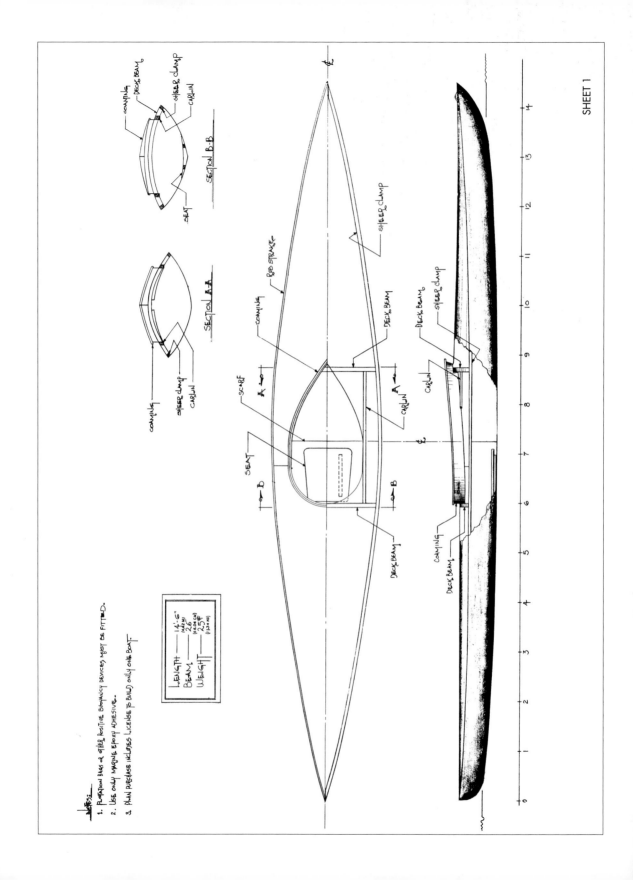

NOTES:

1. PORTABLE BAGS OR OTHER POSITIVE BUOYANCY DEVICES MUST BE FITTED.

2. USE ONLY MARINE EPOXY ADHESIVE.

3. PLAN PURCHASE INCLUDES LICENSE TO BUILD ONLY ONE BOAT.

LENGTH	14'-6" (4.42 M)
BEAM	26" (66.04 CM)
WEIGHT	25# (11.34 KG)

SECTION B-B

SECTION A-A

SHEET 1

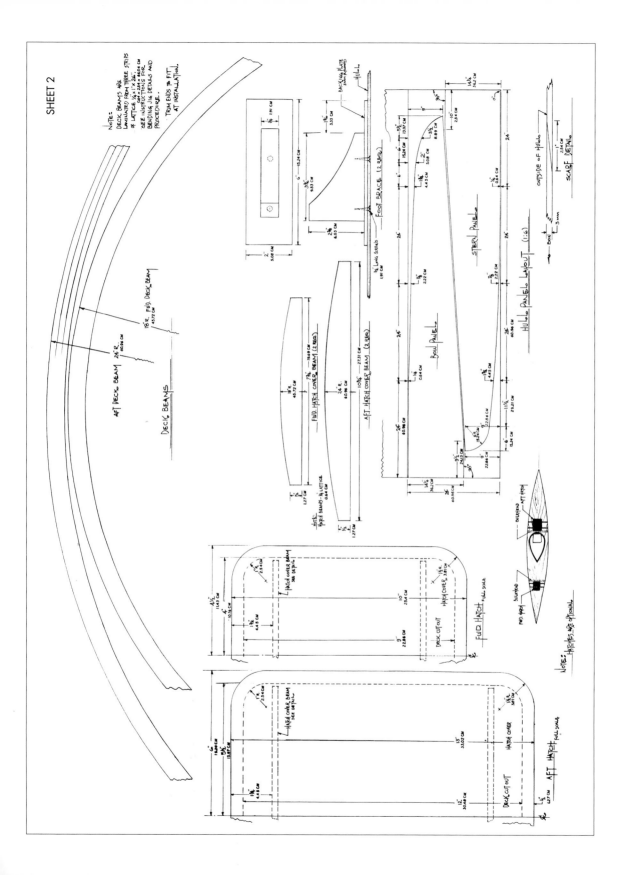

SHEET 2

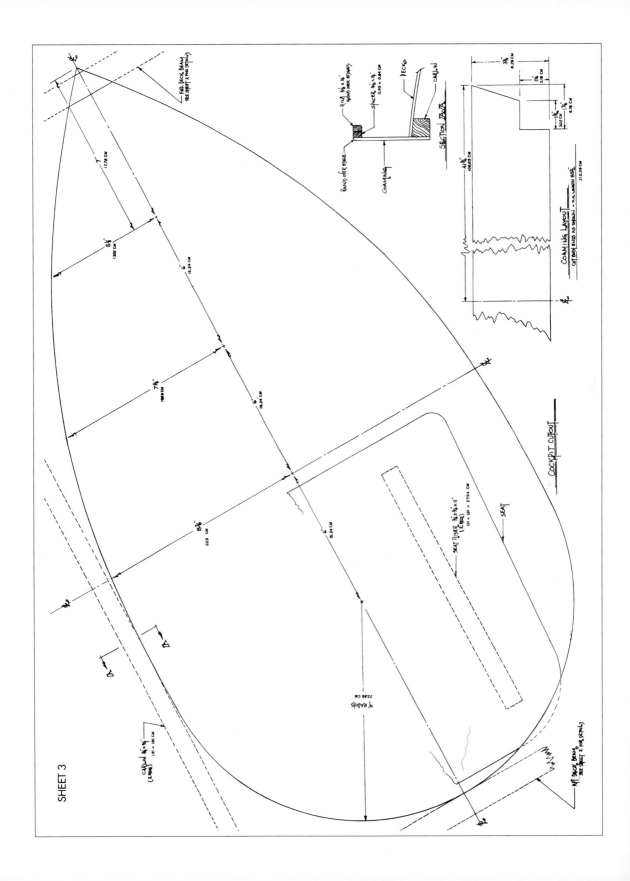

SHEET 3

An ultralight flatwater kayak, the pretty little Severn weighs only 26 pounds. Though it is meant for smaller paddlers, I can squeeze my more than 200-pound frame into the Severn for a test paddle.

(continued from page 67) okoume: there is a tremendous bend and twist in its hull, and inferior plywood will crack when bent to this hull shape.

SEVERN BILL OF MATERIALS

- 2 sheets 3 mm BS1088 okoume marine plywood
- ½ sheet 6 mm BS1088 okoume marine plywood
- 36 feet of ¾- by ½-inch spruce, fir, or other strong, light wood
- 6 feet of ¾- by ¾-inch spruce, fir, or other strong, light wood
- 32 feet of ¼- by ½-inch mahogany,

oak, teak, or other tough decorative wood
- 8 feet of ¼- by ¼-inch ash, white oak, or other easily bent wood
- 1.5 gallons catalyzed marine epoxy
- silica thickening agent for epoxy
- wood flour thickening agent for epoxy
- 5 yards of 6-ounce, 38-inch-wide fiberglass cloth
- 25 feet of 18-gauge bare copper wire

- 8 #10 1-inch bronze screws and finish washers
- 8 #8 1½-inch bronze wood screws
- 4 ounces of ¾-inch, 15-gauge bronze ring shank nails
- 12 feet of shock cord
- 24- by 24-inch sheet ¾-inch Minicel foam
- backband
- footbraces

CHAPTER SIX

Making the Hull Panels

Boats are composed of curves. For many woodworkers this is a daunting fact. After all, you can't just slap down a straight-edge and draw a curve. But a few tricks make laying out the curved lines of the hull panels less difficult. When building a hard-chine boat, such as the Chesapeake, you can even get away with slight errors in your layout. On the other hand, the panels of multi-chine boats and compounded-plywood boats, such as the West River and the Severn, must be laid out and cut exactly right if they are to "bend up" properly.

In building the Chesapeake and the West River, plywood blanks are joined with a scarf joint prior to laying out and cutting the hull panels. The plans show

the size of these blanks. The exact placement of the scarfs is not important so long as the resulting blanks are large enough to contain the hull panels. If you have plywood left over from another project or cut to odd sizes, feel free to work out your own layout scheme.

In building the Severn, all four hull panels are cut from a single sheet of plywood and then joined to form two long panels with a scarf joint. It's easiest to first lay out both panels on one half of the plywood sheet, then rip it in half, stack the two halves, and cut the panels out in pairs. I'll discuss making scarf joints first, then layout, so you'll need to reverse the order of these steps if you build the Severn.

73

Four hull panels are lined up on the edge of the workbench prior to cutting the scarfs. Each step in these 4 mm panels is 1¼ inch wide.

If you plan to build from a precut kit, you can skip most of this chapter. Your panels and scarfs will have been cut, so you'll need only to align and glue them.

Scarf Joints

Since kayaks are generally longer than sheets of plywood, you'll need to join two or more pieces of plywood. The best and most elegant way to accomplish this is to make a scarf joint, which is simply two overlapping bevels glued together. The idea behind a scarf is to provide large surfaces for the glue to bond. If the length of the joint is at least eight times the thickness of the wood to be joined, then a properly glued joint will be as strong as the surrounding wood. I've purposely broken numerous scarfed panels to see whether the

scarf was a weak point; in all instances the surrounding wood cracked first.

CUTTING A SCARF USING A BLOCK PLANE

Start by marking the inside edge of the scarf to be cut with a pencil line; if you imagine the scarf as a "ramp" up to the full thickness of the panel, this line marks where the very top of the ramp should fall. Since you'll be cutting an 8:1 scarf, this line will be 1 inch from the edge to be scarfed when joining 3 mm plywood (3 mm multiplied by 8 is 24 mm, or about 1"). For 4 mm plywood, an 8:1 scarf would be 1¼ inch wide. Line up the edge of the panel to be scarfed flush with the edge of your workbench. If the edge of your workbench is chewed up and scarred, first tack down a good surface, such as a piece of scrap plywood.

The simplest way to cut a scarf is with a block plane. Before you start, make sure that your plane is sharp by trying it out on a piece of plywood. Don't just feel it with your finger. The glue in plywood quickly dulls plane irons, so you might need to resharpen the plane after you've cut a few scarfs. Set your blade for a shallow cut. It might seem that you're saving time by planing off great swaths of wood all at once, but sooner or later you'll tear out a big chunk and perhaps ruin the panel.

TOP: *Cutting the scarf. Notice that the plane is held at an angle of about 45 degrees to the panels.* **BOTTOM:** *The finished scarf shows a parallel pattern of veneers.*

An overlapping bevel, or scarf, is the best way to join thin plywood panels.

Plane away the wood between your pencil line and the bottom edge of the panel where it meets the edge of your workbench. Hold the plane at a slight angle and slowly cut along the edge of the plywood. As the "ramp" is formed, the layers in the plywood will appear as bands; try to keep these bands parallel as you plane. When you have a smooth, flat surface between your pencil line and a featherlike edge against the workbench you're done.

It is both easier and faster to cut scarfs on as many as four panels at once. Position the panels flush with the edge of your workbench. Slide the top panel back so that its edge rests on the pencil line of the panel below it; stagger all the panels that you're scarfing in this way and clamp them to your workbench. Now you can cut a ramp between the pencil line on the top sheet and the edge of the workbench, just as you would with a single sheet.

Cutting scarfs with a block plane is probably easier to do than it is to explain. Practice on a piece of scrap and you'll soon get the hang of it.

OTHER WAYS TO CUT SCARFS

Cutting scarfs with a block plane is simple and convenient. But professional boatbuilders, who must be very efficient to make a living, have come up with several timesaving methods for cutting them. If you decide to build more than one kayak, one of these methods is worth trying.

I've cut many scarfs with a belt sander. The technique is similar to using a block plane. Mark the edge of the scarf and

Cutting scarfs with a belt sander. The paper must run down the panels.

stagger the panels at the edge of your bench. Sand away the wood to form a ramp instead of planing it away. Hold the sander so that the belt runs down the ramp, not up it or sideways to it, to prevent tears. It's easy to sand off too much wood, so work slowly. An 80-grit sanding belt seems best for cutting scarfs.

I've also cut scarfs using a router and jig. The router is fitted with a wide mortising bit and mounted on a short board. The board, with the attached router, slides up and down a frame set at the proper angle to cut an 8:1 scarf. The frame or jig fits over the plywood panel to be scarfed, and you need only push the router along to cut it perfectly. The only drawback is that setting everything up can take as long as cutting the scarf with a plane or belt sander. Of course, a production shop could dedicate a router and table exclusively to scarfing and have an almost perfect system.

You can also use a scarfing attachment made by West System for a circular saw that cuts scarfs on panels up to ⅜ inch thick. The attachment consists of a guide that holds the saw at the proper angle to the panel. The guide rests against a straightedge clamped to the panel. Although this system is fast, the setup time is considerable, it won't handle several panels at once, and the finished scarf is rather rough-looking compared with scarfs cut using the other methods.

GLUING SCARFS

Though I've rarely heard of one failing, you should always be extra careful when gluing scarf joints. Check that the temperature is within the epoxy manufacturer's specifications, that the resin and hardener are mixed to exactly the right ratio, and that the panels are perfectly aligned.

If you start from precut panels, as you'll do if you build the Severn or if you build from a kit, the alignment of the panels is critical. Make a baseline or stretch a string line on the surface where you'll glue the panels (see illustration page 78). Lay the panel above the baseline and check at least three offsets. Check one offset near each end and one near the center of the panel; they should match the plans. You might also trace the proper alignment of the panel on the work surface so that it will be easy to see any slippage of the panels while the scarfs are being glued. If gluing blanks, simply use a long straightedge to make sure that they are straight.

Place a piece of wax paper or plastic film under the scarf. Mix an ounce or two of epoxy and thicken it with silica powder to the consistency of jam. Spread epoxy on both surfaces of the joint. Carefully position the bevels and check that the resulting plank is straight by stretching a string line beside it. Clamp or staple the pieces to the workbench or floor to prevent their shifting when the joint is clamped. The pressure of clamping a scarf joint often causes the joint to slide apart, so it's important to secure the panels first. Cover the joint with a second sheet of wax paper or plastic.

Clamping a scarf joint can be tricky. With narrow panels or solid wood strips, ordinary C-clamps will do the job. Be sure to place a wooden pad over the joint to spread the load of the clamp. Don't overtighten the clamps; some epoxy should

Aligning precut panels (such as the Severn's) with a string line.

squeeze out of the joint, and the surfaces should touch, but too much pressure will squeeze all the epoxy from the scarf, making a weak joint.

Many panels will be too wide for C-clamps—the jaws of the clamp cannot reach far enough into the panel. The easiest way to secure wider panels is to use staples or drywall screws. Lay a strip of thin scrap plywood over the wax paper–covered joint and drive a staple every inch or so along the joint. The staples must be long enough to pass through the scrap strip and the scarf and into the surface they're resting on (not your hardwood

floor, I hope). I use the long staples intended for installing acoustic ceiling tile. Tap each staple with a hammer to ensure that it's fully driven. After the epoxy has cured, pull up the scrap strip and the staples. More than one panel can be stacked and glued this way as long as you have staples long enough to penetrate them; you can fill the tiny staple holes with a mixture of epoxy and wood flour (see illustration page 80). If the hull is to be painted, you can use small drywall screws instead of staples. Just place a scrap of thicker wood, at least ½ inch thick, over the joint and drive a screw every 6 inches.

ABOVE: *Masking a scarf joint with wide adhesive tape prior to gluing saves sanding later. The excess epoxy can simply be peeled off with the tape.* RIGHT: *An alternate way to clamp scarfs in narrow panels is with a board and drywall screws driven into the workbench. Be sure to coat both faces of the scarf with epoxy.* BOTTOM: *Another way to clamp scarfs is with a heavy weight, such as a 5-gallon bucket of water.*

If you're a perfectionist, the idea of little staple holes in your boat may not appeal to you. In this case, clamp your panels by placing heavy weights on top of the joints; full 5-gallon buckets of water make good weights. Place the panels on the floor or table and secure the ends so the panels don't slide apart when weight is placed on the joint. Position a piece of wax paper and then a block of scrap wood on the scarf. The wooden block should be slightly larger than the joint; that way all the weight will be concentrated on the joint. Finally, balance the weight on the block and double-check that the panels have not slipped out of alignment.

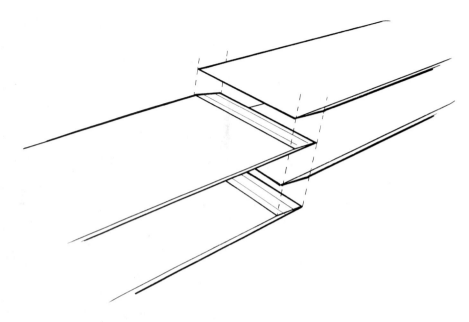

Several scarfs may be glued on top of each other. Use wax paper or plastic between the panels.

Harbor Sales in Maryland can scarf sheets up to 50 feet long, but how do you get them home?

Most scarf joints will require a little sanding to remove the glue that's squeezed out of them. Sand the joint carefully so that you don't remove any wood.

COMMERCIALLY SCARFED PANELS

Your plywood supplier may be able to scarf two or more panels for you. Harbor Sales, of Sudlersville, Maryland, produced a plywood sheet 50 feet long for a U.S. Naval Academy rowing barge, probably the longest sheet of plywood ever made in America. And they will make a longer sheet if the customer can figure out how to get it home. The scarfed sheets from Harbor Sales are nicely done and inexpensive, but how does one economically ship a 16- or 20-foot-long panel? If you live near a supplier that can deliver scarfed panels, or if you own or can borrow a large truck, it might be worth considering commercially scarfed panels. But for most of us the logistics of transporting them means we'll have to scarf our own.

Butt Joints

Some kayak plans call for butt joints instead of scarfs. Butt joints are simply two pieces glued edge-to-edge with a small piece of plywood, called a *butt block*, or fiberglass tape glued under them to reinforce the joint. In addition to being rather inelegant and heavy, butt joints affect the way panels bend, resulting in a flat spot at the joint.

I believe that some kayak kit manufacturers and designers use butt joints only because they don't want to invest in the custom-made machines required to cut hundreds of scarfs a day. Or perhaps they want to advertise that butt joints are simpler to make. But the fact is that any prudent builder will still check the alignment of the panels, whether the joint is a scarf or a butt, and will secure the panels to the workbench prior to gluing. And the gluing time is the same. So the only possible advantage is to a plan builder who refuses to take an hour or two to learn to cut scarfs.

You'd be hard pressed to find a professional boatbuilder who prefers butt joints to scarfs in boat hulls. For relatively flat areas, such as decks, butt joints are acceptable and may even be preferable, but knowledgeable builders prefer scarfs for hull panels.

Laying Out the Panels

Most kayak plans, including the three in this book, contain layout diagrams show-

Here you can see a butt joint and a scarf joint side by side. Notice the flat spot in the butt-joined panel. Don't use butt joints in hull panels.

ing the exact dimensions of the hull panels. Usually these consist of *offsets* from the edge of the plywood sheet or from a baseline. Offsets are measurements at right angles to the baseline or panel edge. In other words, they define points a given distance up the baseline, then a given distance to the left or right of it. They are like the coordinates you learned to use in middle school math class—and thought you'd never use again. The idea is to transfer these measurements to your plywood sheet and then connect them with a curved line.

First, mark the baselines (or centerlines) on the plywood with a long straightedge or chalkline. It's best to work on the floor or on a long bench—you cannot allow the panel to droop off the end of your

TOP: *Offsets are measured along and up from a baseline using a carpenter's square.* BOTTOM: *Small brads hold the batten against the measured points and ensure smooth curves.*

work surface. If you don't have a sufficiently long straightedge, use the factory-cut edge of a second sheet of plywood. When using a chalkline, flick any excess

chalk off of the string as you pull it out of its case; otherwise it will "splatter" when snapped and leave too thick a line. Remember, baselines must be perfectly straight and legible.

Measure down the baseline and mark off the intervals, or *stations*, for each offset. Most of these are spaced at 1-foot intervals, as in our three plans. Now you can mark the offset measurements with a carpenter's square. There will be an offset to the bottom edge and to the top edge of the panel at most stations; mark them both. Use the square to ensure that each offset measurement is exactly at a right angle to the baseline. Always measure from the edge of the chalkline rather than trying to estimate its center; of course, you must always use the same edge of the chalkline. Mark each measured point with a small penciled cross. After you've laid out all the points, double-check them— it's less trouble than ordering more wood if you've goofed.

Next connect the offset points with a *batten*. The batten is a long thin strip of wood that bends in a smooth curve and is used like a flexible straightedge to help you draw the edge of the panel. You can buy special lead weights, called *ducks*, to hold the batten in place, but they work only on gentle curves. A better way is to drive small nails, or *brads*, at each measurement point and hold the batten against these with clamps, a few bricks or rocks, or assistants. Take your time adjusting the batten to ensure a *fair* curve; that is, a curve without any bumps, kinks, flat spots, or hollow areas. The only way I know to judge the fairness of a curve is just to stare down it for a while. When you're satisfied that your batten is lying in a truly fair line, pencil in the curve. If the batten seems unfair, or if it does not touch one of the brads, recheck the offsets.

The curves at the bow and stern of a panel are often shown full-size on the plans. Lay these into position and use an awl or pin to prick through the paper and into the plywood; then remove the paper and connect the dots. If you work from plans in a book or magazine, you'll need to redraw these patterns to full size. Try to be as accurate as possible, although you can usually get away with some small errors in these stem pieces.

Occasionally you'll need to lay out a curve or arc by using a radius given in the plans, as in the Severn's stems. The *radius* of a curve is simply the distance from the center to the perimeter of a circle having the same curvature as the curve. In other words, it's the distance from the point to the lead of a compass drawing that curve. The best tool for laying out a radial curve is a set of *trammels*, a large version of a draftsman's bar compass, which can be found in better hardware and tool stores (see photo page 32). The trammels are clamped to a wooden bar; one trammel holds a pencil, the other a sharp point. The trammels are adjusted to the proper distance apart and used just like a compass. Of course, you can make longer bars, and so can swing larger radii, with trammels than with a compass. If you don't have trammels, drill two holes in a strip of scrap wood and use one for the pencil and the other for a brad driven at the center point of the curve; the distance between the holes is the radius.

Cutting Out the Panels

When you have laid out the panels and double-checked all the measurements, it's time to cut them out. You can use a handsaw, a saber saw, or a circular saw for this. If you use a saber saw, fit it with a fresh 10-tooth-per-inch woodcutting blade. If you use a circular saw, fit a fine-toothed crosscut blade and set the depth of cut to no more than the total thickness of the panels. Wear safety goggles while cutting so you won't be temporarily blinded by a puff of sawdust.

The mirror-image port and starboard panels should be cut out from stacked panels to ensure that they will be identical. Lay the panels on your workbench with the layout line just over the bench's edge. Clamp both panels together so they won't shift as you cut.

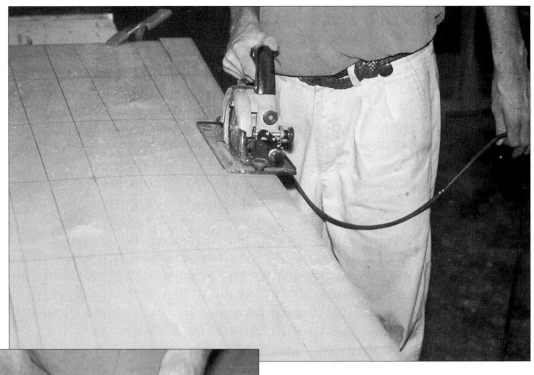

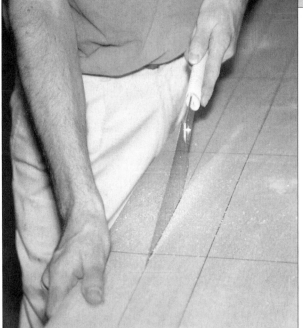

Don't cut the panels exactly to the layout line. If you have a steady hand, try to stay about 1/16 inch outside it; if not, aim for about 1/8 inch outside it. Later you'll trim the panels exactly to the line with a block plane. Allow the saw to find its best speed through the wood; don't try to push it faster than it can cut. You may find it easier to use two hands to guide a power saw. Keep moving the panel on the workbench so it's always supported an inch or so from where you're cutting; if allowed to droop, the resulting panels will not be identical. If you use a circular saw to cut the panels, switch to a saber saw or a keyhole saw to cut the sharper curves at the ends.

I prefer to remove the last bit of wood with a block plane instead of a saw because I'm much less likely to cut beyond

TOP: *Let a power saw find its own speed and cut just outside your layout line.* BOTTOM: *A Japanese saw is a fine tool for cutting out the panels; in this case, the panels will make a West River 180.*

ABOVE: *Use a block plane to trim the planks exactly to the layout lines. Plane the panels in pairs so that they will be identical.* RIGHT: *The finished panels await assembly.*

the line with the plane. And a plane leaves a fairer curve and a smoother edge. It's important to keep the plane sharp and not set too deep. Though this might seem like a tedious step, you can plane the edges of a set of hard-chine hull panels in about 20 minutes.

When you trim your panels, remember that the two sides of the boat must absolutely, positively, and without a doubt be identical. If they aren't, the kayak will pull to one side and you'll spend all your paddling time going in circles. Again, it is critical to support your panels so that they don't droop off the edge of your workbench. If they droop, the top panel will be slightly larger than the bottom panel. Try to keep your plane perpendicular to the panels so that you don't plane more from one panel than from the other. Sight down the panels as you plane, making sure the edge is fair. It's easy to get carried away and plane a flat spot. For this reason it's better to plane to the outside of the pencil line rather than to the inside. When you've finished the panels, lay them on your shop floor and check once again that they're identical.

CHAPTER SEVEN

Stitch-and-Glue Basics

It's time to make all those plywood panels into a boat. Seeing the parts take shape so quickly is exciting. By building these kayaks without hull forms or frames you save a lot of work. But there is the inevitable tradeoff: you must rely on your eye and skills to get the hull's shape right. Of course, the shape of the panels will largely determine the shape of the hull, but you must be sure that the hull does not bend, twist, or deform in some other way as it's being assembled. Having no form to hold the hull's shape or to guide you is not as big a problem as it might seem. If you stand back and look at the hull every once in a while, you'll detect any problems that might be creeping in. Most folks have a better eye for symmetry and shape than they realize. Just don't forget to look.

In this chapter we'll go over the basics of wiring the hull together, checking for twist, and joining the panels with epoxy and fiberglass. In the next chapter I'll discuss the assembly of each of our three boats in separate sections. And, once you understand how these three boats go together, you'll be able to figure out most others with little trouble.

Installing the Sheer Clamps

Before joining the hull, glue the sheer clamps in place. Sheer clamps, the two stringers that are usually glued along the

TOP: *This simple table-saw jig cuts scarfs in sheer clamps.*
BOTTOM: *The scarfing jig in use.*

top of the hull, or *sheer*, provide a bonding surface so the deck can be glued to the hull (see top photo page 89.) Bronze ring nails or screws driven into the sheer clamps secure the deck until the epoxy cures. The sheer clamps also provide a

place to anchor deck rigging, hatch hold-down straps, and rudder hardware.

A few kayak designers prefer not to use sheer clamps. While it is possible to join the hull to the deck with fiberglass tape and epoxy, these must be applied from inside the hull, an awkward and sticky procedure requiring brushes attached to long sticks or small children who lack fear of tight places. We'll install the sheer clamps.

The sheer clamps are as long as the top, or sheer, hull panels, which means that you'll probably need to scarf together two or more pieces of wood to obtain the needed length. The Chesapeake and the West River have ¾- by 1-inch sheer clamps, while those in the Severn are ¾ by ½ inch, so you can rip them from a nominal 1-inch board of spruce, fir, or other strong flexible softwood. If you don't have a table saw, pay the lumberyard to cut them for you.

Because these solid pieces are much thicker than plywood panels, the scarfs will be longer. The scarf in a ¾-inch sheer clamp will be 6 inches long, and that in a ½-inch sheer clamp will be 4 inches long. You could cut scarfs in solid wood with a block plane as you did in the plywood panels, but it is faster to cut away most of the wood with a handsaw and finish up the ramp with a plane.

An easier way to cut scarfs in sheer clamps is with a table saw. Make a wooden jig that holds the wood at the proper angle to the blade. The jig must slide with the wood, so it should ride in the saw's miter-gauge groove. With a jig like the one shown in the top photo on page 88, you can cut the scarfs in a set of sheer clamps in just a minute or two. After gluing the scarfs, allow the epoxy to cure for 12 hours, then sand off any epoxy that's squeezed out of the joint.

In the Chesapeake and West River kayaks the sheer clamps should be glued ¼ inch *proud*; that is, ¼ inch of the sheer clamp should extend above the side panel. The Severn's sheer clamps are glued flush with the tops of the panels. Remember that it's the wider side of the sheer clamp that's glued to the hull panel. Also, notice that the sheer clamps on the Chesapeake and West River kayaks stop short of the bow and stern, while those on the Severn extend right to the tips. This is because the bow and the stern of the Chesapeake and the West River will be reinforced with a solid mass of epoxy, called an *end-pour*. To save weight, the Severn's plans call in-

TOP: *On some boats, including the Chesapeake and the West River, the sheer clamps do not extend to the ends of the hull panels.* BOTTOM: *You'll need lots of clamps to install the sheer clamps.*

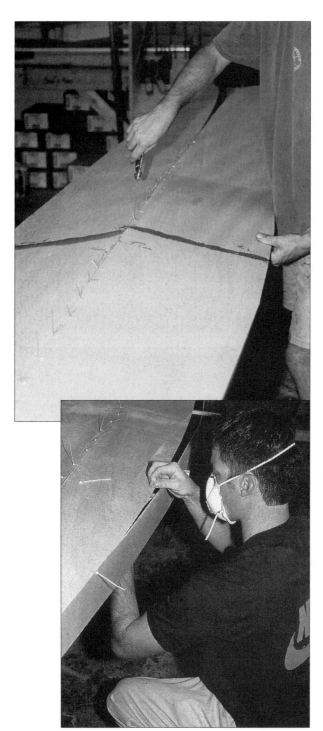

TOP: *Wire ties hold the panels together.* BOTTOM:
*Plastic electrical ties are faster, but they require
larger holes.*

stead for the ends of the sheer clamps to
be beveled later.

I prefer to glue the sheer clamps onto
both hull panels at once. That way you
can compare the positions of the two
sheer clamps as you install them to ensure
that they're identical, and you'll need only
half as many clamps. Start by stacking the
panels back to back, with the sides that
will eventually face outside facing in. Run
a strip of masking tape along the inside
edge of the stack, or the eventual outside
sheer, so that any glue that drips out of
the joint won't cement the two hull panels
together. Spread some thickened epoxy
along the entire length of both sheer
clamps. Position the sheer clamps on the
panels and place a clamp every 6 to 8 inches.
Finally, make sure that the sheer clamps are
on the inside of both panels. Don't laugh
—I've seen more than one boatbuilder
make two left hull sides.

Stitching

The stitch-and-glue assembly method
solves the problem of trying to hold the
hull planks in the shape of a kayak with
conventional woodworking clamps. Short
lengths of copper wire or plastic ties can
be used to hold these large panels in position while fiberglass tape, or cloth, and
epoxy are applied to join them permanently.

The holes for the wires should be
spaced every 3 to 4 inches along the seam
to be joined. They should be a little larger
than the diameter of the wire or tie used:
drill $\frac{1}{16}$-inch holes for 18-gauge wire and $\frac{1}{8}$-
inch holes for the smallest plastic ties.

Drill the holes ¼ to ⅜ inch from the plank's edge. It's best to stack and then drill similar planks together so the positions of the holes will match.

Next, align and stitch the planks together. Cut 3-inch lengths of wire, pass the pieces through the holes, and then twist them finger tight on the outside of the hull. For most hard-chine boats it's easiest to join the stems first, then the keel line, and finally to join the sheer panels to the bottom panels. For a multi-chine boat, first join the keel line, then add the bilge panel, and work up to the sheer panel; join the stems last. In either case, insert all the wires and twist them loosely before concerning yourself about the shape of the hull. It is usually most convenient to have an assistant hold the panel in position so that you can determine its fore and aft placement. Start wiring at either the bow or the stern. Many builders seem to like to stitch the boat upside down, but this is both difficult and slow because in order to insert all the ties you have to squat down to reach under the overturned hull. It's easier on the knees to first insert a tie every 2 feet or so to hold the hull together loosely, then turn the boat over and insert the remaining ties from the top, and then turn the hull upside down again to tighten the wires.

Once all the ties are in place and finger tight, tighten them further with a pair of pliers. Tighten only until the planks touch. Overtightening will pull the wire through the wood or break it. If some areas are difficult to pull together, drill a few more holes and add additional ties. Pay careful attention to the curve of the seam. Is it fair? If not, adjust the ties or remove them and touch up the planks with your

When all the wires are in place, flip the boat right side up and push the wires down with a screwdriver.

plane. Finally, flip the hull over and use a screwdriver point to push down each wire until it lies flat against the inside seam.

On some boats, such as the Severn, as you wire the bow and stern together you'll have to stop and cut a bevel in the sheer clamps so that they'll meet at a point. Mark this bevel by running a chalkline from the point where one sheer clamp meets the tip of the bow to the point where the other sheer clamp meets the tip of the stern panels. Snap the line on both sheer clamps. Cut along the line and along the stem edge of the hull panel. Make this tricky cut carefully with your handsaw; it's better to cut a little proud and then plane the bevel until the sheer clamps fit together perfectly.

TOP: *Mark the sheer-clamp bevel with a chalkline.* **LEFT:** *The ends of the sheer clamps must be beveled in some boats, including the Severn.* **BOTTOM:** *It's important that the panels be perfectly aligned at the bow and stern.*

After you've wired the bow and stern together, check to see that the hull is symmetrical. If the planks are misaligned by even ⅛ of an inch, the boat could pull to one side. Make sure that each pair of hull panels, which you previously ascertained were identical in length and alignment, meet evenly at the bow and stern, that is, that one panel does not extend past its mate. If a panel does stick out, tap it with a mallet. If this does not bring it into position, loosen the wires and slide it back.

Checking for Twist

Occasionally, twist develops in boats built without forms and strongbacks. In the case of a hull that's glued upside down, such as the West River hull, simply placing the boat on two sawhorses that are level and perpendicular to the boat's keel will ensure that no twist develops while you are gluing and glassing. But a boat that is built right side up, such as the Chesapeake or the Severn, must be checked for twist and carefully supported while it's being glued.

A technique called *winding* allows you to quickly check that your kayak is straight. It involves sighting two straight sticks placed across the hull to see that they are parallel. Make a mark an equal distance from the bow and stern (I use 4 feet) and place two straight sticks at least 3 feet long across the hull exactly on these marks; you must be accurate in this. Stand a few feet from the bow and stern and sight down the boat. Line up the bow and stern as if they were rifle sights and squat down until the two sticks appear to touch. It should be easy to see whether the winding sticks are parallel or askew. If they are askew, adjust the hull's supports to remove the twist. In more severe cases, have an as-

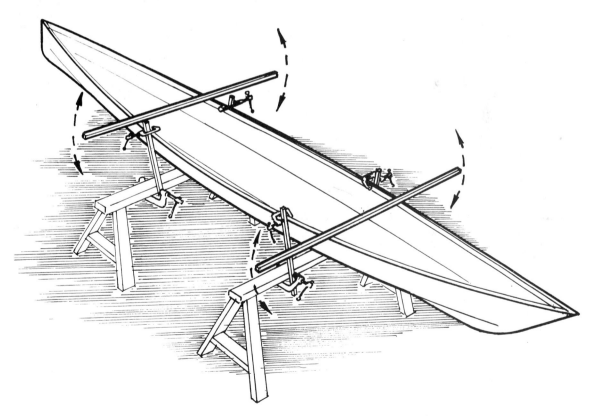

Winding is a technique for checking twist in a hull.

CONSERVING EPOXY

Many first-time boatbuilders use more epoxy than is necessary. Epoxy is both expensive and heavy, so here are some tips to help you use less of it, spend less money, and build a lighter boat.

- Mix small batches. Large batches of epoxy have a shorter pot life than smaller batches because the heat generated during curing isn't dissipated as effectively. Mixing smaller batches will help ensure that the epoxy won't *kick*, or harden, prematurely, leaving you with a hockey puck of wasted glue in the bottom of your mixing cup.

- On flat surfaces apply thin coats of epoxy with a short-nap, yellow-foam roller. This will help prevent runs and sags. Not only will you save epoxy but you'll save a lot of sanding as well.

- Once the weave of fiberglass cloth is full or almost full, don't apply more epoxy. It will add little or no strength, just extra weight.

- Plan your epoxy use. If you're gluing several small parts, have them all lined up and ready before mixing the epoxy so it won't cure in the cup while you're preparing the next part.

- Use enough epoxy in joints, but not too much. When you clamp a joint, a little epoxy should squeeze out. But epoxy running and dripping out of the joint is wasted.

sistant hold one end of the hull while you "untwist" the other. A variation of this technique that's handy in small shops where there is no room to sight down the boat is to use two carpenter's levels. Don't get carried away with winding though; in most cases minor twist, of ¼ inch or less, has no effect on the boat's performance. In fact, a surprising number of commercially manufactured kayaks have a slight twist.

After winding, check again to see that both stems are vertical and that there are no distortions, twists, lumps, or hollows in the hull; this is your last chance.

Fillets

A fillet is a thick bead of epoxy at the inside juncture of two parts. The fillets, along with the fiberglass covering them, form structural members that are much like chine logs or stringers in traditional wooden boats. They also cove out the sharp inside corner and allow fiberglass cloth to lie against it. (By the way, the boatbuilding term "fillet" is pronounced "fill-it," not "fill-lay" as in a slab of fish.)

The size of the fillet is determined by the thickness of the plywood and the angle between the plywood panels being joined. A good rule of thumb is to make the fillets at least as thick as the plywood being joined. But tight corners, such as the keel area close to the stems, require much thicker fillets if fiberglass tape or cloth is to lie smoothly over the joint.

When mixing epoxy for fillets, use fillers that absorb the glue. Wood flour is inexpensive and makes a stiff and strong paste. Its dark brown color also looks nice

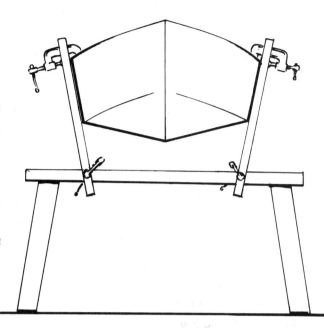

ABOVE: *Securing the kayak while making fillets.*
RIGHT: *Fillets join the panels.* BOTTOM: *Removing the excess epoxy before it hardens is very important.*

on a wooden boat. By adding a little white filler to the mix, you might even match the plywood color. Some fillers, such as silica powder, are held in suspension in the epoxy and should not be used alone when making paste for fillets. Even though the paste made with this sort of filler appears to be quite stiff, it will flow out of the joint. Some builders, however, do add a little silica powder or microballoons (no more than 30 percent by volume) to the wood flour to make a smoother or lighter fillet mix.

Remember to mix the epoxy resin and hardener thoroughly before adding the thickening powder. Make a paste that has the consistency of peanut butter—smooth not chunky—and spreads without "pulling." If the epoxy is too stiff,

ABOVE: *A selection of homemade filleting tools will help you make neat fillets.* LEFT: *Apply fiberglass tape to the fillets while they are still wet.*

precoat the joint with unthickened epoxy to ensure that a dry joint won't weaken the hull. Since epoxy will heat up and harden quickly in a large mass, get the mixed epoxy out of the container quickly. Distribute lumps of epoxy along the seam to be joined.

One secret to making good fillets is having the right tools—simple spreaders cut from thin plywood or from inexpensive putty spreaders (available in any auto-parts store). Make an assortment of tools like those in the photo above. The longer spreaders are particularly useful for making fillets in the narrow bow and stern sections of kayaks. Some builders use light-

Wet out the fiberglass tape and coat the entire inside of the kayak with unthickened epoxy.

bulbs, soupspoons, or lids from jars as spreaders.

Use the spreaders to push the epoxy along the joint. Carefully scoop up any material that squeezes past the sides of the spreader. It's important to scrape up any epoxy that's not part of the fillet; remove excess epoxy now instead of sanding it off later. It is difficult to make a neat fillet in the tight confines of the kayak's stems; fortunately, no one will see this area once the deck is in place.

Apply fiberglass tape to the fillets while they are still wet; if the fillets are allowed to harden, they must be sanded smooth prior to applying the tape. Simply lay the fiberglass tape over the fillet and smooth it out, but take care not to deform your perfectly contoured fillet. The width and weight of the tape used, as well as the number of layers required, will be specified in the boat's plans or assembly manual. Adding additional tape to the inside of the hull will do little to strengthen it; however, extra layers of tape may be added to the outside of the hull to provide abrasion resistance.

Wet out the tape with unthickened epoxy. Use a disposable bristle brush to work it into the fiberglass, being careful to eliminate any air bubbles and dry spots. Also, brush a coat of epoxy onto all the wood inside the hull to seal it; mix more epoxy as needed.

Glassing the Hull

I recommend sheathing, or glassing, the outside of all stitch-and-glue kayak hulls with fiberglass cloth set in epoxy. Glassing the hull greatly strengthens it and increases its resistance to abrasion.

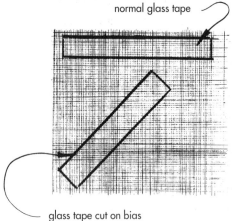

normal glass tape

glass tape cut on bias

TOP: *Drape a single piece of fiberglass cloth over the entire hull.* **BOTTOM**: *Fiberglass cloth cut on a 45-degree bias makes a flexible patch for the bow or stern.*

Prior to glassing the hull, pull out or cut off all the ties. In multi-chine hulls there are few fillets, so the wires can be cut and pulled out with pliers. But the large fillets in hard-chine hulls make the wires difficult to remove, so it's easiest to cut them off flush with the wood. Most builders use diagonal-type wire cutters to cut ties; however, these leave a tiny nub of exposed wire that should be removed with a file or sanded flush with the wood. One well-known stitch-and-glue boatbuilder advocates removing all wires because they may eventually loosen and poke through the fiberglass cloth. I've neither seen nor heard of this happening in any of the many thousands of my boats that have been launched. But should you prefer to remove all the wires, heat them with a plumber's torch to soften the surrounding epoxy and then pull them out with pliers.

Once you have cut or removed the wires, sand off any epoxy that's dripped through the joints. Sand a smooth radius on, or *round over*, all hull joints; fiberglass will not lie flat over sharp corners. On hard-chine boats the stems and chines should have a radius of ⅛ to ³⁄₁₆ inch, which is about as rounded as a fountain pen or a thin cigar. On multi-chine hulls the chines should be lightly sanded to eliminate sharp corners, but the stems must be generously rounded.

You may notice small gaps between the panels on the outside of the hull. Fill these with "epoxy peanut butter." Use a plastic squeegee to trowel a bit of paste into the joint and then clean off the excess with the edge of the squeegee. It's important to clean up any excess epoxy; keep reminding yourself that it's easier to wipe off uncured epoxy than to sand it off after it's hardened.

Lay a sheet of fiberglass cloth on the overturned hull. Smooth the cloth by pulling it gently toward the sheer. The cloth will stretch to conform to the curve at the bow, but on some boats you may need to cut a slit and overlap the cloth, or add a second piece of cloth, at the stern. I like to add a second layer of fiberglass at the stems. This patch is cut on the bias, or at a 45-degree angle to the weave, as shown in the sketch opposite. Bias-cut cloth is stronger since more fibers cross the sharp stems, and it is easier to make it conform to the shapes of the bow and stern. Bias-cut fiberglass is sold by fiberglass suppliers, but it's easier and cheaper to cut your own from a scrap piece of regular fiberglass.

Mix up about 12 ounces of epoxy and pour all of it out along the boat's keel. Quickly, before it all runs onto the floor, start spreading with a squeegee (see top photo page 100). Pull the epoxy down the hull and toward the sheer. Work from the center toward the edges to avoid wrinkling the cloth. Mix and pour more epoxy as needed. But use only the minimum amount of epoxy required to saturate the cloth; don't "float" it by applying too much epoxy. Use the squeegee to squeeze out excess epoxy from under the cloth. The surface should be smooth and dull; white areas indicate too little epoxy, while shiny areas and bumps indicate too much.

When the epoxy is no longer sticky, cut off the cloth hanging below the sheer with a utility knife. Then roll on a second coat of epoxy to start filling the "pattern" in the glass. Use a foam roller to apply this second thin coat; again, try to avoid drips and runs. It's best to recoat epoxy within a couple of days as this will ensure a strong chemical bond. In fact, you can recoat as soon as the epoxy has started to "gel." If you wait more than 48 hours, lightly sand the hull before recoating. It usually takes two to four coats of epoxy to fill the weave of the cloth. Many builders find that lightly sanding the hull after the second coat results in a much smoother finish and saves considerable sanding later. Be careful not to sand into the cloth, though. You will see the cloth's fibers if you cut into it, so stop sanding every few minutes to check that you've not gone too far down.

Continue rolling on thin coats of epoxy until most of the pattern in the cloth has disappeared; it's OK if a few areas of weave show, but most of the hull should be smooth and shiny. Don't apply any more epoxy than is needed to fill the

weave; it won't increase the strength of the boat, but it will add weight.

Making End-Pours

The bow and stern tips of many wooden kayaks are filled with plugs of solid epoxy called end-pours. If the boat is to be fitted with hatches, the end-pours may be made after the deck is in place, but it's almost as simple to do it now. Tape over the last 6 inches or so of the hull with duct tape or packing tape, as shown in the lower photo. Stand the boat on end by leaning it against a tree or building. Mix about 8 ounces of epoxy and add a little thickener to bring it to a syruplike consistency. Pour it into the end of the boat and allow it to harden. Flip the hull end for end and repeat the process. Be sure to use only slow epoxy hardener when making an end-pour; fast hardener, because of its large mass, will cause the mix to boil.

TOP: *Use a squeegee to glass the outside of the hull.* BOTTOM: *End-pours reinforce the ends of the hull. Notice that the bow is sealed with plastic packing tape.*

CHAPTER EIGHT

Assembling the Hull

Now that you understand how a stitch-and-glue hull is assembled, we'll apply these techniques to our three boats.

Assembling the Chesapeake's Hull

After installing the sheer clamps, place the side panels sheer clamp to sheer clamp. Drill several ⅟₁₆-inch holes 4 inches apart and about ⅜ inch from the edge along the stems, or ends, of the panels. Wire the bow and stern together loosely with short pieces of copper wire. Use a piece of scrap wood as a spreader stick to bring the panels to their eventual beam of 23½ inches. Remember that beam is measured at the outside, not the inside, of the hull.

Start wiring the Chesapeake's hull by laying the bottom panels on the overturned side panels. A few scrap sticks across the side panels temporarily support the bottom panels. Put in a wire or plastic tie every 2 feet or so.

101

ABOVE: *It's easiest to insert most of the ties with the boat right side up.* **LEFT:** *Turn the hull over again and adjust the wires.*

Drill a wire hole ⅜ inch from the edge every 4 inches along both the inside and outside edges of the bottom panels. Stack the panels before drilling so that the holes will be in identical positions on the two panels.

Loosely wire the bottom panels together along their inside edges. Place the side panels upside down and then place the wired-together bottom panels on top of them. Center the bottom panels between the ends of the stem curves and drill a hole in the side panel to correspond with each hole in the bottom panel. Now loosely wire the bottom panels to the side panels. It's easiest to begin by inserting a wire only every 24 inches or so, then flip the hull right side up to insert the remaining wires, and flip the hull over again to tighten all the wires. Now you can see the shape of your hull.

Turn the hull right side up again and push the wires down inside the hull with a screwdriver point so that they lie flat against the wood. Tighten or loosen the wires and adjust the position of the panels until the joints are smooth and even, with no lumps or hollow areas. Remember that the panels should touch along their inside corners. Bumps along the seams may be caused by a high spot on the panel edge; if this is the case, you may need to remove a few wires and plane down the offending panel edge. Low spots can be fixed by inserting a matchstick or splinter between the panels to bring them to the proper position.

Carefully support the hull so that there's no distortion where it rests on saw-

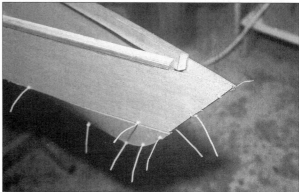

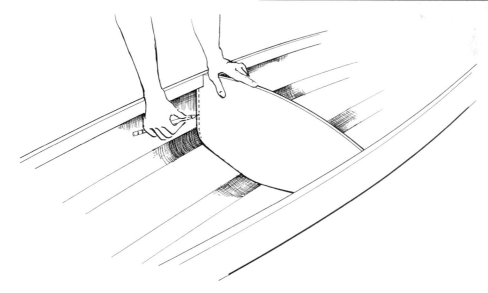

TOP: *Small wooden wedges spread the keel seam where it was not quite fair. Of course, the wedges will be cut flush with the panels.* MIDDLE: *Double-check to see that the panels meet perfectly at the bow and stern before epoxying the hull.* BOTTOM: *Scribing the bulkheads. Cut bulkheads a little large and insert them into the hull where they happen to fit. Then use a pencil held against the hull to scribe the exact shape required. Recut the bulkhead to the pencil line, check the fit, and rescribe if necessary.*

horses or the workbench. Four blocks of wood positioned just under the chine make a good support, or you can hang the hull. Mark the widest point of the kayak at the sheer. The distance from the bow to the widest point of the hull is 104 inches, and the maximum beam at the sheer at this point is 23½ inches. Check that the spreader stick brings the hull to exactly this beam. If these measurements are true, the hull will assume its proper shape. Near the point where the four panels join at the bow and stern the bottom panels may tend to flatten out. If this happens, use a spring clamp to squeeze them into a sharp V; the bottom panels should be almost vertical for the last 3 inches. Check the hull for twist.

Make a neat fillet along each joint so that it just covers the wires. Cut a length of fiberglass tape and lay it over each fillet. Mix about 16 ounces of unthickened epoxy and brush some of it over the tape to saturate it. Cut a piece of fiberglass cloth to the shape of the bottom panels and lay it over the bottom of the cockpit area (between the bulkheads) while the epoxy is still wet. Saturate the cloth as you did the tape. Take care to use only as much epoxy as is needed to wet out the fiberglass tape and cloth. Excess epoxy pooled along the keel can contribute several pounds to the weight of your kayak.

Wire the bulkheads into position as shown on the plans. The bulkheads should fit loosely so they don't distort the shape of the hull. Trim or sand the bulkheads for a good fit and apply small epoxy fillets around their perimeters. (See illustration page 103 and top photo page 105.)

When the epoxy has hardened, gently turn the hull over and cut the wire ties off flush with the plywood. Scrape or sand any epoxy that has squeezed through the joint. Sand or file down the remaining ends of the copper wire. Fill any gaps between the panels with thickened epoxy. Round over the chines, keel, and stems to allow the cloth sheathing to lie smoothly.

Cover the outside of the hull with fiberglass cloth as described in chapter 7. Finally, make end-pours in the bow and stern.

Assembling the West River's Hull

Begin by drilling wire holes around the perimeter of the bottom panels, 6 inches apart and about ¼ inch in from the edge. Starting at the bow, loosely wire the bottom panels together along the keel line. Twist the wires on the outside of the hull, but don't tighten them. Starting at the bow again, drill holes in the second set of panels that correspond to the holes in the bottom panel. Loosely wire the second pair of panels to the bottom panels. Next, drill holes along the top edge of the second pair of panels and drill corresponding holes along the bottom edge of the third pair of panels. Loosely wire the third and then the fourth pair of panels into position. With all the panels wired together along their lengths, drill two holes along the bow and stern edges of each panel and wire them together along the stems.

Cut a spreader stick and insert it between the sheer clamps to spread the hull to 22 inches; remember, that's on the outside of the hull. Wire the bulkheads into

position as shown in the plans. If you weren't accurate in your cuts, you may need to adjust the shape or position of the bulkheads slightly. It's always better for the bulkheads to fit loosely rather than too tightly so they don't distort the hull's shape; epoxy will fill any gap between the bulkhead and the hull.

Tighten all the wires holding the hull together. Tighten or loosen the wires and adjust the position of the panels until each joint is smooth and even, without lumps or hollows. This is your last chance to check the shape of the hull, so take the time to make sure that all the panels are as perfectly joined as possible.

Make an epoxy fillet around each bulkhead. Also make a larger fillet inside the stems. Use a long stick to reach into the pointy end of the hull to glue the panels together. Shape and smooth the fillets and scrape up any excess epoxy.

Turn the hull upside down on two

TOP: *The bulkheads fit loosely so as not to distort the hull.*
BOTTOM: *Wire the West River from the keel outward. Leave the stems until last.*

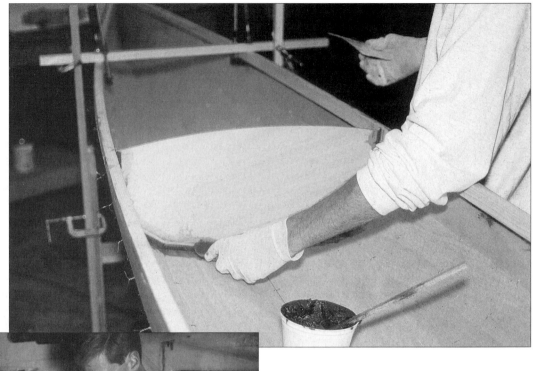

level and parallel sawhorses. Place the sawhorses next to the bulkheads to ensure that there will be no twist in the hull. Fill the gaps between the panels with thickened epoxy using a squeegee. When the epoxy has hardened, turn the hull over, cut the wires, and pull them out. The wires along the stems may be difficult to remove; simply cut these off flush with the plywood. Finish filling the seams on the outside of the hull, including the spots behind the wires.

Lightly sand the hull smooth and clean up the joints. Round over the stems with your sander so they form a smooth radius. Glass the outside of the hull as described in chapter 7.

Cut pieces of fiberglass cloth to fit into each of the three compartments inside the hull. The cloth should reach to just below the sheer clamp. Sand the in-

TOP: *Make a neat fillet along both sides of both bulkheads.*
BOTTOM: *Also make a fillet in the West River's stems.*

side of the hull lightly. Lay the cloth into the hull and saturate it as you did on the outside. Work the wrinkles out by "pushing" them up toward the edges of the cloth. It's easier to cut separate strips of cloth for the stems. It's not necessary to fill the weave of the cloth inside the hull, though some builders may wish to do this in the cockpit area for aesthetic reasons. Finally, make end-pours as described in chapter 7.

Joining the Severn's Hull

The Severn's is the trickiest of the three hulls to join. Since this hull has no chines to keep it rigid while it's being joined, the builder must "eyeball" the proper shape. And when the hull planks are first being taped, they bear little resemblance to the final hull shape.

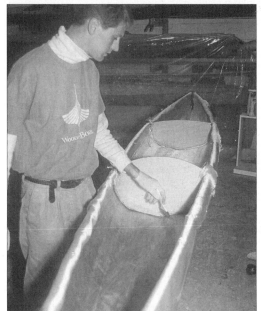

TOP: *Tab the hull by filling the seams between the panels with thickened epoxy.* MIDDLE: *After removing the wires, glass the entire outside of the hull.* ABOVE: *The inside of the West River's hull gets a layer of fiberglass.*

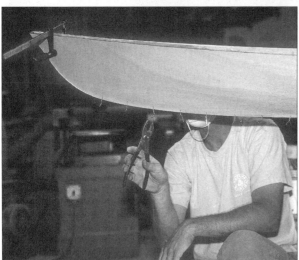

TOP: *Wire the Severn's hull with the panels supported on two sawhorses.* BOTTOM: *Tightening the wires.*

inch intervals along the keel line, ¼ inch from the edge. Lay the two hull planks, sheer clamps up and keel line to keel line, on your sawhorses so that they touch at the scarf. The sawhorses should be about 2 feet from the ends of the panels. The center 8 feet of the two panels will be wired together and taped first. You may notice that the panels don't touch for the full 8 feet. If, however, you push down near the center of the planks, they will bend into a U and will come together along the entire 8-foot length. At this stage the hull will look more like a miniature skateboard ramp than a kayak, yet this is the position in which it will be glued and taped. It doesn't seem possible that the hull should be joined while in this ridiculous position, but trust me—it will work.

Wire the panels together for 48 inches to either side of the scarf. Twist the wires loosely on the outside of the boat while pushing the planks down. The planks must be almost flat across the scarf joint when they are taped. You can hold the panels in this alignment by making and using an alignment jig. Place it on the scarf joint and clamp the sheer edges of the planks to it. Cut this jig from scrap ¾-inch board. The sheer should be 1 inch above the keel; the jig will hold the panels at the proper shallow V. The ends of the panels, still supported by the sawhorses, should now be at least 2 feet higher than the center part of the hull, which droops between them. And there should not be a bump or hollow at the jig; rather, the keel line should describe a smooth curve from sawhorse to sawhorse.

Tighten the tie wires so that the two

Start by sighting down the keel line of the panels one last time. It is critical that the keel line be a smooth, fair curve, so touch it up if necessary. When you are satisfied, start drilling tie-wire holes at 3-

panels touch along the entire 8-foot length. It's particularly important in the case of the Severn that the center seam run in a smooth curve without any bumps, flat spots, or hollows. I'll say it again: even a slight imperfection will be greatly magnified when the hull is pulled together. So check again, and don't hesitate to cut the wire ties and touch up the panel edges with a plane or sandpaper if they aren't perfect. A few extra minutes spent getting this seam just right can save you lots of work later on.

Two layers of fiberglass tape on the inside and one on the outside of the panels will form the Severn's keel. Make a small fillet over the wires. Lay 8 feet of fiberglass tape over the seam. Mix up about 8 ounces of epoxy, but don't thicken it. Saturate the tape with epoxy. Lay a second, 7½-foot piece of tape over the first

TOP: *It may look odd, but this is how the Severn hull will look when it is ready for epoxy.* BOTTOM: *Gently flip the hull panels over and tape the keel seam.*

EPOXY IN COLD WEATHER

When fall arrives, the leaves start to turn, farmers harvest their pumpkins, we dig out our pile jackets, and epoxy companies' tech lines light up with complaints about their products not curing. I usually recommend using a slow-cure epoxy hardener because it's much easier to use than a fast hardener. But what's slow in summer is glacial when the temperature drops. So what do you do if you have only an unheated work space?

- If at all possible, find, borrow, or build a heated space. Or if your shop is insulated, get a space heater. Epoxy is formulated to work at room temperature, so this is your best option.

- Order some fast hardener from the epoxy manufacturer; it will let the epoxy harden in much colder temperatures. But be warned that fast hardener is more likely to form amine blush, so be sure to scrub the boat before painting or overcoating.

- Keep epoxy containers in a heated space even if the boat is not. Keeping the resin warm will make it easier to mix and apply. It will also prevent your calibrated dispensing pumps from failing because warm epoxy is thinner and therefore easier to pump.

- After applying the epoxy, drape a plastic tarp over the boat and aim a small space heater under it. Even on a cold night you can bring the small airspace under the tarp up to room temperature. But be very careful not to let the heater touch the tarp and start a fire. Even a lightbulb will raise the temperature under a tarp by a fair amount.

- Finally, rest assured that the epoxy, if properly mixed, will eventually harden. Unfortunately, that might not be until spring.

and saturate it. Once the epoxy has hardened, turn the boat over, sand off any epoxy that's dripped through, and apply an 8-foot piece of tape over the outside joint. Allow the epoxy to cure overnight before proceeding.

Now it's time to wire together the bow and stern sections of the boat. As you pull the hull together it will start to assume its final shape. It may also seem that your boat will explode at any minute—there's a lot of stress on the thin plywood at this stage. This is where the little bit extra you spent on the good stuff pays off! But just to be safe, wet the area around the end of the tape and along the keel with water; this is the area of greatest stress, and occasionally the plywood will crack here. Remove the jig at the scarf, pull the ends of the panels together, and wire them to-

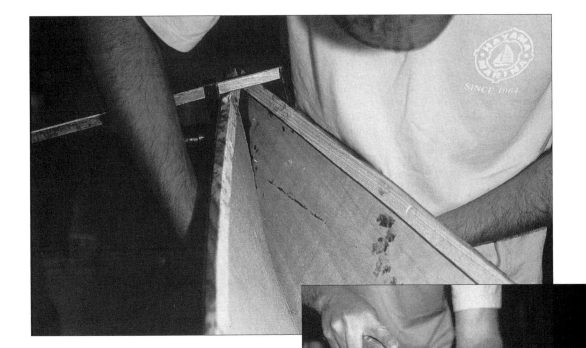

gether. Pull the hull together until the maximum beam is 25 inches; hold it at this beam with pipe clamps or string. Cut the bevels in the sheer clamps at the bow and stern so that they meet in a point. (For more on cutting sheer-clamp bevels, see pages 91–92).

One of the problems with this method of construction is that it can be difficult to eliminate a bulge that often forms in the keel line where the center section of tape ends. If you can't squeeze the seam shut at this point, cut the original tape back along the seam for about 3 inches. Use a hacksaw blade to cut a slit a few inches long, then pass a few additional wire ties through the tape to pull the seam shut. Occasionally a Severn hull will have a concave dip along the seam. This occurs when the hull planks have been planed too flat, and can be repaired by slitting the

TOP: *Pull the hull together by adding wires; work from the middle toward the stems.* BOTTOM: *Cut the bevel with a handsaw.*

taped seam along the affected area, pushing it out slightly, and taping it again. You may need to jam a splinter of wood or a wooden matchstick into the seam to keep it in position while you retape it.

Make a fillet and apply fiberglass tape

to each end section of the hull seam. The fillet should be at least deep enough to cover the tie wires. Lay the tape over the still-wet fillet; it should overlap the center tape by a few inches. Use a thin piece of wood or a disposable brush to push the tape and epoxy into the narrow ends of the hull.

When the epoxy inside the boat has cured, turn the hull over, cut off the tie wires, and sand or scrape off the epoxy that has dripped through the joint. It's also a good idea to sand off the raised edges of the tape now. Finally, glass the outside of the hull with 4-ounce cloth.

Note that I don't make end-pours in the Severn. This is to cut down on the weight of the boat and because a flatwater kayak doesn't need to be as strong as a sea kayak.

CHAPTER NINE

Installing the Deck

The deck is what you see when you're paddling, and it's what others see first when they look at your boat. You'll certainly want to varnish it to show off the wood, so try especially hard to do a neat job of installing it. A minor flaw on the hull can always be hidden with a little fairing compound and a good paint job, but every scratch, dent, and tear in the deck will show.

Fortunately, since you have already completed the hull, your woodworking skills are tuned up, and installing the deck is easier than building the hull. Installing the deck is an exciting step: you'll finally get to see what the finished boat will look like. And though there's still a lot left to do, it'll all seem downhill once the deck is in place.

Before installing the deck you'll have to install the structure that gives it shape and support. This includes making and fitting deck beams, bulkheads, and carlins, and planing the tops of the sheer clamps. You may also want to install backing plates for footbraces, a sailing rig, a diaphragm-type bilge pump, or other accessories before the hull is buttoned up.

The Deck Beams

The deck beams are structural members that span the hull from sheer to sheer. They support the deck and coaming, help hold the hull at the proper beam, and add rigidity to the kayak. The deck beams for

113

our three kayaks are curved, or *cambered*, like the decks. They are made by laminating strips of wood over a jig. The strips can be cut from thin spruce or pine or from leftover 3 or 4 mm plywood.

The radius of a deck beam describes its curvature. A smaller radius gives the deck a higher camber; a larger radius makes a flatter deck. The radii of the deck beams for our three kayaks are shown on the plans. If you didn't spend middle school geometry class drawing boats in your textbook, as I did, you may remember that a radius is simply the distance between the center and the outside edge of a circle or arc.

If you want to increase the volume of your kayak or gain extra knee room, you can decrease the radius of the deck beams slightly, though the appearance of the boat will change. For decks on single kayaks I prefer a 15- to 24-inch radius forward and a 24- to 48-inch radius behind the cockpit. The transitional area between the two different deck cambers worries some builders, but the flexibility of okoume plywood allows them to blend together very smoothly. Of course, the camber of the deck does not have to be radial; you could draw it as a section of a parabola, a combination of two radii, or any smooth curve for that matter. The deck beams should be about ¾ inch thick for single kayaks and about 1 inch thick for doubles.

Making the Deck Beams

You can make a simple bending jig like the one shown in the photo below in just a few minutes. First, draw the required ra-

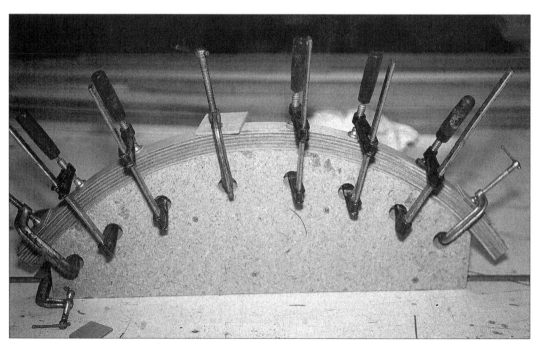

This simple jig is used to laminate the deck beams.

dius on a piece of ¾-inch-thick scrap board; remember that if the radius shown on the plans is to the top of the deck beam, you must subtract the thickness of the beam to find the radius of your jig. Because the deck beam will spring back a little when removed from the jig, I like to cut the radius 1 inch smaller than shown on the plans. For example, if the plans call for an 18-inch radius at the deck, the deck beam is 1 inch thick, and we want to allow an extra inch for spring-back, then we'd cut the jig with a 16-inch radius.

The easiest way to draw the radii is with a set of trammels. If you don't have a set, drill two ¼-inch holes in a piece of thin scrap wood; the distance between the holes should be the same as the radius. Insert a pencil into one of the holes and a nail into the other; using the nail as the center of the arc, swing the pencil around it to draw the radius. Of course, most plans have full-size drawings of the deck beams that can be traced directly onto the jig. Cut the board along this arc. Finally, drill large holes for the clamps about an inch below the curved edge.

Another way to make a jig is to screw blocks of wood to the board along the radius line. A jig of this type is a bit more trouble to make but it's easier to keep the wood strips aligned on it; if you'll be building several boats, it's worth the extra effort.

Cut strips of plywood or solid wood to the size required for the deck beam. Make the deck beam a few inches longer than required; it will be trimmed later. Thinner strips are easier to bend and clamp onto the jig and cause less spring-back. Solid wood strips make a stronger deck beam than plywood strips because all the wood's grain is oriented along the long axis of the beam. If you make plywood strips, the grain on the surface should run along the beam's long axis.

Lay the strips on a piece of plastic sheeting and spread thickened epoxy on the surfaces to be joined. Stack the strips and wrap them in the plastic so they won't stick to your jig. Clamp the strips onto the jig as shown in the photo opposite and allow the epoxy to cure overnight. Make sure that the epoxy is hard before removing the deck beam; you should not be able to dent the epoxy with your fingernail. Scrape, sand, or plane off any epoxy that has squeezed out from between the strips. Round over the inside corners of the deck beam.

Installing the Deck Beams

With the hull clamped at the proper beam, mark the fore and aft positions of the deck beams on the sheer clamps. Hold the deck beams on the sheer clamps in their eventual positions and mark their lengths. The angle of the cut can be determined by holding a straightedge to the inside face of the sheer clamp: draw this angle on the side of the deck beam, as shown in the photos on page 116. Since the sheer clamps angle inward, cutting the deck beam to the lines you just drew would result in too long a beam. You could simply keep shortening the beam until it fits, but from long experience I can tell you that if you cut ¼ inch inside each mark, the deck beam's length will be very close to perfect.

TOP: *Mark the deck beam's length while holding it on the hull.* BOTTOM: *The deck beam is installed by passing screws through the hull and sheer clamp and into the end of the deck beam.*

Glue and screw the deck beams into place at the positions you marked. The screws should pass through the sheer clamps and into the ends of the deck beam. Predrill the holes for these screws so

that they won't crack the sheer clamps. The screw head should be flush with the surface of the hull.

Installing the Carlins

Carlins are essentially deck beams that run fore and aft. They strengthen the area around the cockpit, and on some designs they provide a surface to which the coaming is glued. They run between the deck beams or bulkheads at the edge of the cockpit cutout. Carlins are rarely used on single kayaks with laminated coamings, but they are required on the Severn, which has a bent-plywood coaming. Many doubles, particularly those with open cockpits, require carlins.

Glue the carlins into place so that the top edges are level and the sides vertical.

The deck beams and carlins installed in a Severn.

You can use long, thin screws passing through the deck beams to hold them in place, or clamp them into position. Don't be too concerned with getting a perfect joint here, or, for that matter, with the deck beam–to–sheer clamp joint; the deck itself acts as a flange to reinforce these joints. After the epoxy has cured, plane the tops of the carlins to follow the curve of the deck beams.

Planing the Sheer Clamps

The angle between the deck and the hull of a kayak is not a perfect 90 degrees, but the corners of the sheer clamps are. Therefore, the top edges of the sheer clamps need to be planed to allow the deck to follow a smooth curve from gunwale to gunwale. The angle between the deck and the hull is not constant but varies over the length of the sheer clamps.

I can imagine you novice woodworkers shaking your heads wondering what I've gotten you into; relax, there's a trick to it. I admit that even an experienced boatbuilder might have trouble planing a rolling bevel such as this one strictly by eye. But if you had a template with the same curve as the underside of the deck you could see exactly how much wood needed to be planed off and at what angle; then it would be simple. Consider that the radius of the underside of the deck is, of course, the same as the radius of the top of the deck beams or bulkheads. So make your

A template with the same radius as the underside of the deck is used as a guide in planing the sheer clamps.

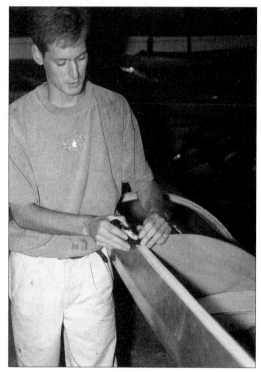

Use long, even strokes when planing the sheer clamp.

template by tracing the deck beam's radius onto a piece of cardboard or scrap plywood and cutting it out. Hold the template across the hull on the sheer clamps and judge how much wood to plane off. Plane some of it off, try the template again to be sure you haven't planed too much, and so on until the sheer clamps match the template. Don't worry if you need to plane away some of the side panel—that's normal.

Since the forward and aft deck beams and bulkheads have different radii, you'll need two templates. With them you'll be able to plane the sheer clamps between the cockpit and the ends of the hull. But what to do about the area alongside the cockpit? Well, the short sections of sheer clamp between the deck beams, near the cockpit, can be easily planed by eye once the bow and stern portions of the sheer clamp are planed. Sight down the tops of the sheer clamps, keeping your eye just above them; you'll be able to easily judge the bevel required to connect the fore and aft sections. One last tip: the camber of the deck usually ends about a foot from the tip of the bow and stern, so the last foot of the sheer clamps is planed flat.

Many first-time builders are intimidated by this step, but it is really quite simple if you have a sharp plane, and should take no more than 30 minutes. And if it's not perfect, epoxy is great for filling gaps.

Cutting Out the Deck

If you studied the plans, you may have wondered if I'd forgotten to give dimensions for the decks. I left them off because it's easier to use the completed kayak hull as a template to mark the deck's shape.

Both the forward and aft deck sections are cut from a single sheet of plywood, so you'll have to draw them end for end on the sheet. Place the plywood on your hull and bend it over the deck beam, then trace the shape by reaching under it. The forward and aft sections of the deck should meet at the widest part of the cockpit; this results in the shortest possible seam between the two large deck panels. So mark the location of the joint on the top of the sheer clamps prior to tracing the deck panels.

Unless you're a professional wrestler, holding the plywood down while drawing on its underside will require an assistant. Have your assistant hold the plywood against the sheer clamps, bulkhead, and deck beam while you trace the hull shape onto it. Do this for both the forward and aft deck sections. The panels should overlap by an inch or two where they'll be joined at

ABOVE: *It's easiest to have an assistant hold the last sheet of plywood in place while you mark the deck panels.*
LEFT: *Seal the underside of the deck with unthickened epoxy, but install the deck while the epoxy is still soft.*

the cockpit; you'll trim them to make a perfect joint later. Since you'll have to bend the deck down again while attaching it, ask your helper to stick around. If you can't find someone to help you, use tie-down straps (the type used for cartopping) to hold the plywood on the hull.

Some longer boats, including the Chesapeake and the West River 180, require a third section of deck scarfed onto the bow. Mark the shape of this, leaving enough extra for the scarf joint, but don't attach it until after you've cut out the main sections.

Cut the deck sections about an inch larger than your scribe lines indicate. If you're building the Chesapeake, the West River, or other long kayak, scarf the extension onto the foredeck; this extension should also be oversized. Finally, cut the cockpit opening a few inches undersize.

It's best to seal the deck's underside and all parts of the inside of the hull with epoxy before installing the deck, or else you'll have to crawl into the bow and stern later. Coat everything with epoxy applied with a foam roller. Coat the deck just prior to installing it; if the epoxy is allowed to harden, it will stiffen the wood and make bending the deck difficult.

Installing the Deck

The deck and hull will be held together primarily by the epoxy in the hull-to-deck joint. But until the epoxy cures they must be mechanically joined or clamped. You could use the stitch-and-glue method to hold them together, but you'd have to drill through the sheer clamps. An easier way is to drive nails or screws into the sheer clamps. I prefer bronze ¾-inch, 14- or 15-gauge ring nails, which have excellent holding power and very thin heads that can be driven flush with the plywood deck. They're easy to use and make a nice pattern on a bright-finished deck. I can live with the few extra ounces of weight they add.

Screws can also be used to hold the deck down. However, the heads of most screws are so thick that they will completely penetrate the thin deck if they are driven flush and thus provide only mar-

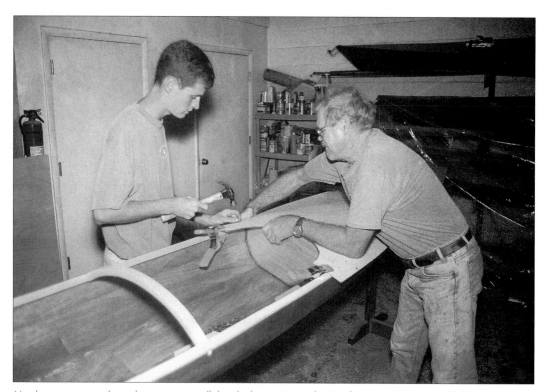

Use bronze ring nails and epoxy to install the deck; again, it's best to have an assistant hold the panels in place as you nail.

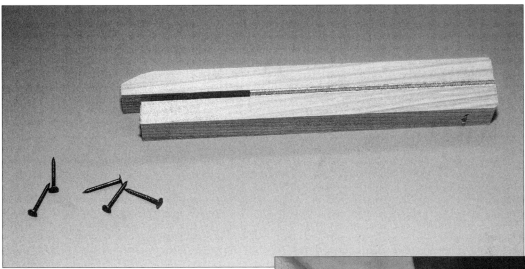

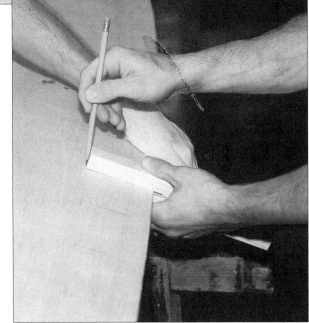

TOP AND BOTTOM: *This homemade gauge helps position the nails over the center of the sheer clamps.*

ginal holding power. One solution is to use pan-head screws and then remove them after the epoxy cures. The holes they leave must be filled before finishing. Using temporary screws is probably only worth the trouble if you're striving to save every possible ounce of weight in a racing boat. If you prefer not to use screws or nails, the deck can be "clamped" with duct tape or with tie-down straps. Since these methods are slower and more difficult, I strongly recommend using nails on your first boat. Some woodworkers, particularly furniture and cabinet builders, object to leaving fasteners exposed, but in boatbuilding it is perfectly acceptable.

Start installing the deck by spreading thickened epoxy on top of the sheer clamps, deck beams, bulkheads, and carlins that will be covered by the aft deck. Position the aft deck panel on the hull. Try to place the deck panel squarely into position rather than sliding it around until it's aligned and smearing thick epoxy all over the underside. Be sure that the deck rests firmly on the deck beam before you begin to fasten it into place. Some builders fasten a tie-down strap around the hull at the aft bulkhead or deck beam to hold the deck and bend it to the proper camber.

Begin fastening at the deck beam or bulkhead just behind the cockpit and

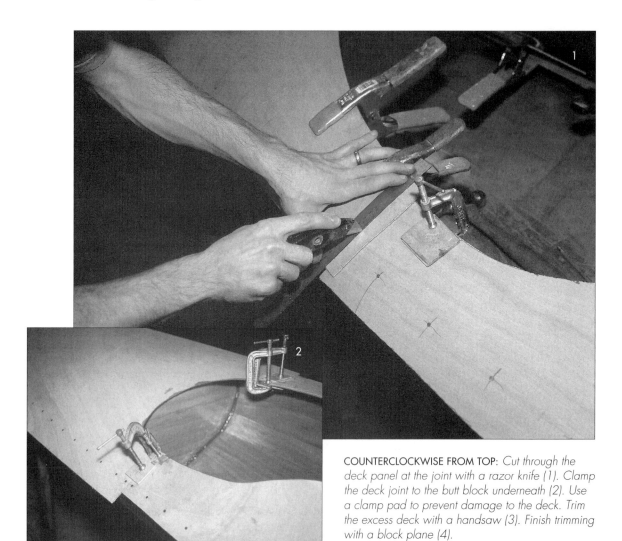

COUNTERCLOCKWISE FROM TOP: *Cut through the deck panel at the joint with a razor knife (1). Clamp the deck joint to the butt block underneath (2). Use a clamp pad to prevent damage to the deck. Trim the excess deck with a handsaw (3). Finish trimming with a block plane (4).*

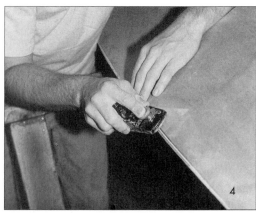

work toward the stern, alternating between the port and starboard sides. The nails or other fasteners should be placed about 4 inches apart, but take care to locate them directly across from each other. If possible, have an assistant bend the deck into position as you drive the nails. After you reach the stern, go back and drive nails from the aft deck beam or bulkhead toward the center of the boat, but do not yet drive the nail closest to the center deck joint.

With the aft deck panel fastened down, spread thickened epoxy on the sheer clamps, deck beams, bulkheads, and carlins under the forward deck. Lay the forward deck panel on the hull so that it overlaps the aft deck section by an inch or two. There's no need to scarf the two main deck panels; a butt block under this joint will reinforce it.

Again, start nailing at the point of greatest curvature, the deck beam just forward of the cockpit. Use a strap or have an assistant bend the deck into position as you nail toward the bow. Make sure that the deck touches the forward bulkhead, if you have one.

With a razor knife, cut through the aft deck panel where the forward deck overlaps. It will take a dozen or more passes with the knife to cut the plywood. Pull out the cut-off section of the aft deck and nail down the forward deck. There should be no gap between the deck panels. Glue a small scrap of wood, or butt block, to the underside of the joint to reinforce it.

After the epoxy in the hull-to-deck joint hardens, cut off the excess deck with your handsaw or saber saw. Cut the deck so that a ⅛-inch overhang remains, and finish up by trimming this with a block plane. It is also possible to trim the deck flush with a router, but, remember that the hull-to-deck joint is not a 90-degree angle. So use a router only if you're experienced with this tool and have a steady hand.

Finishing the Hull-to-Deck Joint

The hull-to-deck joint can be finished by simply rounding over the corner or by adding a rubrail.

Today, most kayaks are finished with a rounded hull-to-deck joint. Start by using a block plane to roughly round the joint. Watch the plies in the edge of the plywood much as you did when scarfing: try to keep the layers even and of constant width. Finish up the joint with a sander. Any small gaps that remain between the hull and the deck can be filled with thickened epoxy.

A kayak's hull-to-deck joint can take quite a beating, particularly when the boat is being transported. A solid wood *rubrail*, or *rubbing strake*, protects this joint and makes an attractive trim piece. But I've found that the rubbing strake serves another, equally important purpose: when you are paddling in a chop, it deflects water that would otherwise climb on deck, and so makes for a drier ride. If you look at a powerboat's gunwale you'll see that others have found the same benefit.

Mahogany, ash, teak, or white oak

make pretty rubrails. Select a piece with a straight grain and rip it, or have it ripped, into ¼- by ½-inch strips. Shorter pieces can be joined into full-length strips with scarf joints. Spread thickened epoxy on the strip and tack it into place with ¾-inch brass brads, one every 4 inches or so. By the way, make sure that the brads are in fact made of brass; some brads are only brass-plated and will rust. Cut the rubrails flush with the bow and stern and taper them, as shown in the sketch below, for a refined look.

Other Types of Decks

Some kayak designs call for decks made from flat sections of plywood. Usually the forward deck is peaked. There may be a flat section at the bow and two sections forming the peak just forward of the cockpit, or the entire forward deck may be composed of two triangular pieces that meet in the

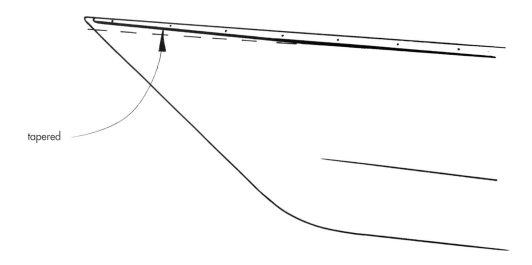

tapered

TOP: *A rubrail protects the hull-to-deck joint and makes an attractive trim piece.* BOTTOM: *Taper the rubrails at the bow and stern for an elegant appearance.*

center. These pieces are usually stitched and taped together. The aft deck may also be peaked, but more often it's simply a single flat sheet. I see no advantage to these types of decks.

Occasionally you'll see a cloth deck on a plywood-hulled kayak. These are usually made of aircraft Dacron or of canvas stretched over a framework of thin wooden members attached to the sheer clamps. Cloth decks can be very pretty, and they are quite light. But they require more work to install than plywood decks. If you decide to install one, read George Putz's excellent book, *Wood and Canvas Kayak Building*.

CHAPTER TEN

The Coaming, Hip Braces, Hatches, and Footbraces

Adding the coaming, hip braces, hatches, and footbraces turns your big empty hull and deck into a kayak. Give these parts the attention they deserve; they directly affect comfort and performance. Even the best hull in the world won't be fun to paddle if the hatches and sprayskirt leak or the footbraces are in the wrong place.

Laminated Plywood Coamings

The size of the coaming is important for comfort. It's nice to be able to raise your knees while sitting in your kayak yet still brace them under the deck, particularly on long trips. Try to buy a sprayskirt that fits so you don't have to make one.

Most sea-kayak coamings are laminated from plywood. Two or three *spacers* are glued to the deck, and a wider rim is glued to them, as shown in the plans. This type of coaming holds a sprayskirt securely, is durable, and can be made almost any size. The coamings I've drawn for the Chesapeake and West River kayaks are a good size for all but the very largest paddlers. They include knee braces to make rolling and bracing more secure. You can, however, easily modify the coamings shown in the plans. You can redraw the cockpit to make it longer, though I wouldn't recommend making it more than 36 inches long. You could make it

127

TOP: *Spread thickened epoxy on all the coaming parts prior to installation.* **BOTTOM:** *Start clamping the cockpit at the boat's centerline.*

wider or narrower, or you might eliminate the knee braces or reshape them. Of course, you'll need to move the forward deck beam if you alter the length of the cockpit, but that's simple enough. A word of caution: if you're not an experienced paddler, stick to the cockpits on the plans.

Use the full-size drawings in your plans to lay out the spacers and the coaming ring, or if you're working from this book, redraw the coamings full-size on the plywood. You'll need two sets of spacers if you use 9 mm plywood, three sets if you use 6 mm wood. Cut each spacer in two pieces to save wood; lay out the two halves so that they "nest." Cut slowly and accurately; sloppy cutting will result in hours of extra sanding after the coaming is glued in. Cut the one-piece top ring or rim from 6 mm plywood. If you tend to abuse your kayaks, sheath the rim with fiberglass cloth to increase its strength.

Run a string line from bow to stern and make pencil marks to help you center and align the cockpit. Position the coaming rim on the deck. It should rest on the forward deck beam and on the aft bulkhead or deck beam. If you use an aft bulkhead rather than a deck beam, the inside edge of the coaming rim should be ½ inch forward of the bulkhead. Tracing the inside edge of the rim on the deck will help you position the spacers.

Spread thickened epoxy on both sides of the first spacer and position it on the deck. Near the end of each spacer drive a brass brad through the deck to hold it in position. Install the remaining spacers in the same way. Place the coaming rim on the top spacers and clamp everything into place. It's important to start clamping at the centerline of the boat and work toward the sides to avoid cracking the rim. Use pads of scrap plywood between the clamps and the rim to avoid denting it. Wipe up any epoxy that squeezes out under the rim so that your sprayskirt won't catch on gobs of hard epoxy later. Make sure that the spacers and rim are neatly aligned, loosening the clamps and tapping the spacers into position with a mallet if required. Finally, peer under the rim to check for gaps.

When the epoxy has cured, remove the clamps and trim the portion of the deck panel that protrudes into the cockpit. If you weren't precise when you cut and aligned the pieces, there will be lots of sanding to do before the inside is

It will take about 2 hours of sanding to smooth up a laminated coaming.

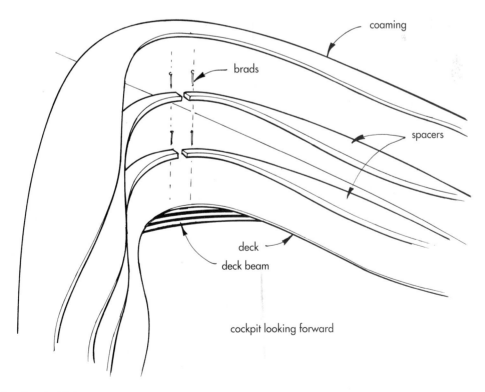

Use brads to hold the coaming pieces in position.

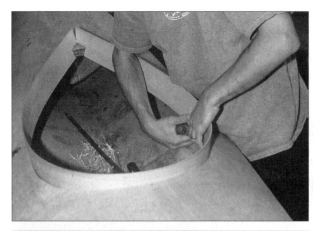

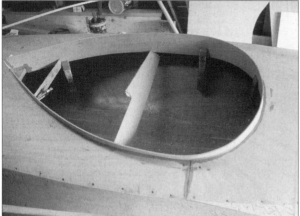

TOP: *Check the fit of the cockpit coaming and adjust it as needed.* MIDDLE: *Scraps of plywood wedged across the cockpit and clamps on the carlins hold the coaming while the epoxy cures.* BOTTOM: *The Severn's cockpit coaming rim is made from two layers of thin, flexible wood.*

smooth and even. Bending the spacers and coaming ring to the camber of the deck causes a slight stairstep effect along the inside of the coaming. A spokeshave will make short work of smoothing this, as will a random-orbital sander, but the final sanding will require some elbow grease. Plan to spend at least two hours sanding the coaming. Don't forget to round over the inside and outside edges of the cockpit rim. When you're finished, the inside of the opening should show a handsome pattern of plywood layers—and you should be ready for a cold beer. But before you retire, brush a coat of epoxy onto all the exposed edges of plywood around the coaming; after it has soaked in, brush on a second coat.

Bent-Plywood Coaming

The Severn's coaming is made from a single, 3¼-inch-wide strip of 3 mm okoume plywood bent around the perimeter of a teardrop-shaped cockpit opening. It is glued to the deck beams, carlins, and deck and reinforced with a fillet of epoxy under the deck.

Start by cutting the cockpit opening. Since this must be quite accurate, make a full-size template from heavy paper and trace the shape onto the deck panels, then cut the opening with a saber saw or keyhole saw. Sand the cutout smooth to eliminate gaps between the deck and the coaming. Next, cut the plywood coaming strip and bend it into place inside the cockpit opening. If the strip is difficult to bend or if you fear that it might crack, wet the wood first, and then clamp it into position and allow it to dry overnight. When the strip is dry, glue it to the carlins and deck beams. A few strips of scrap wood wedged across the cockpit and some clamps at the carlins and deck beams will hold the coaming strip tight against the deck until the epoxy cures. Apply an epoxy fillet along the underside of the deck-to-cockpit coaming joint to reinforce it.

The Severn's cockpit rim is made of two thin strips of wood glued to the top edge of the coaming. The strips should be ¼- by ⅜-inch ash or other easily bent wood. It might be wise to soak these too. Glue them into place and cut a bevel where they meet at the front.

When I first built this style of coaming I was unsure how strong it would be and considered laminating a second layer of plywood inside the first. But the single layer of 3 mm plywood has held up for 8 years now, so I guess it's strong enough. You could also apply a layer of fiberglass cloth to the inside and outside of the coaming to increase its strength.

Glue the completed bent-plywood coaming to the deck, carlins, and deck beams.

Hip Braces

Hip braces prevent the paddler from sliding off the seat when bracing or rolling. Hip braces for the boats described here can be simple wooden uprights on either side of the seat, part of a commercially available seat unit, or cut from thick, closed-cell foam and glued into the boat.

The simplest hip braces are trapezoids of 6 mm plywood, as shown in the plans. Sit in the boat and determine where the hip braces should be positioned; remember

that you'll probably pad them with ⅜-inch foam later. Cut the hip braces to the correct height and glue them into position at the edge of the seat and under the deck just outside the cockpit opening. Hip braces must be strong, so reinforce them with an epoxy fillet at both the top and the bottom. Foam hip braces are best cut from 3-inch-thick Minicel foam. Cut them with a bandsaw or a keyhole saw and sand them smooth, but don't glue them into place until the cockpit has been varnished. If you purchase a seat with built-in hip braces, simply install it according to the manufacturer's instructions, as you would in a fiberglass kayak.

Hatches

Hatches give access to the areas behind the bulkheads, allowing convenient storage of camping gear or whatever you might like to take along. Most hatches are not completely waterproof; the hatches I've designed for my boats aren't. In fact, the vast majority of hatches on plastic and fiberglass kayaks are not completely waterproof either. This isn't as tragic as it sounds since prudent paddlers keep most of their gear in waterproof dry bags. Though the few ounces of water that find their way past most hatches during a day of paddling will not noticeably affect the kayak's buoyancy, they will definitely ruin your new Nikon. It's always safer to assume that any hatch will leak, so keep cameras, sleeping bags, and clothes in dry bags. A little water on your tent is not a big deal, but finding your toilet paper wet can ruin your evening.

If you insist on truly watertight hatches, you can install those ugly plastic inspection plates on deck. Actually, it's a better idea to install them in the bulkheads; since you can't get much gear through them, you might just as well put them where they won't be seen. Or you can use the excellent though equally ugly and very expensive British VCP rubber hatches. These are available as kits consisting of the hatch cover and a rim; they are intended for installation on fiberglass kayaks, but they can be adapted for use on a wooden deck. (See opposite, top.)

The hatch covers used for all of my boats are similar in design. They are simply plywood covers to which small frames are glued to give them the same camber as the deck. Wide weather stripping glued to the perimeter of the hatch cover seals the hatch cover to the deck. Nylon straps screwed to the deck and sheer clamps hold the hatch covers in place. Your plans should contain full templates for the forward and aft hatch cutouts; if you are using the plans in chapter 5, you'll have to redraw them full-size. You may want to redraw the hatches to change their size and shape, but I've found that I can easily fit my winter sleeping bag, the biggest item I carry, through the aft hatch and my tent through the forward hatch; larger hatches would be of little benefit and would weaken the deck.

Start by drawing a light centerline on the deck in the area of the hatches. The aft hatch should be far enough back for a paddle blade to fit between it and the coaming, thus allowing an easy paddle-float-assisted wet reentry. Place the forward hatch just ahead of the forward bulkhead. Line up the centerlines on the templates with the centerline on the boat and trace the cutouts. Drill a starter hole for the blade of your saber saw or keyhole saw, then cut out the openings. Glue a strip of wood about 2 inches thick along the fore and aft edges of the opening. These stiffeners should span from sheer clamp to sheer clamp under the deck. Clamp them as shown opposite (bottom).

Make the frames for each hatch cover from short pieces of thick plywood or softwood by tracing the curve and cutting them to shape. The frames should just fit into the deck opening and should match the camber of the deck. Check them against your deck and sand them to fit if necessary. Glue the hatch frames onto the bottom of the hatch covers with thickened epoxy; use a clamp at each end of each frame. Take care that the hatches don't twist when you clamp them.

After saturating the hatch covers with epoxy and then varnishing them (see chapter 12), glue foam weather stripping along the perimeter of the hatch cover as shown on page 134 (middle). Use the thickest, widest, and softest weather stripping you can find; ¾- by ⅜-inch closed-cell foam, self-adhesive weather stripping is best.

After varnishing the deck, attach the hatch straps to the sheer clamps with 1-inch #10 screws and finish washers. Fold about an inch of each strap under as shown in the bottom photo on page 161 and melt the screw hole in it with a nail

TOP: *Inspection ports in the bulkheads are an alternative to deck hatches if you plan to carry only small items. They are available at marine stores.* BOTTOM: *The hatch stiffeners fit athwartship under the fore and aft edges of the hatch cutouts. They strengthen the deck, so don't leave them out.*

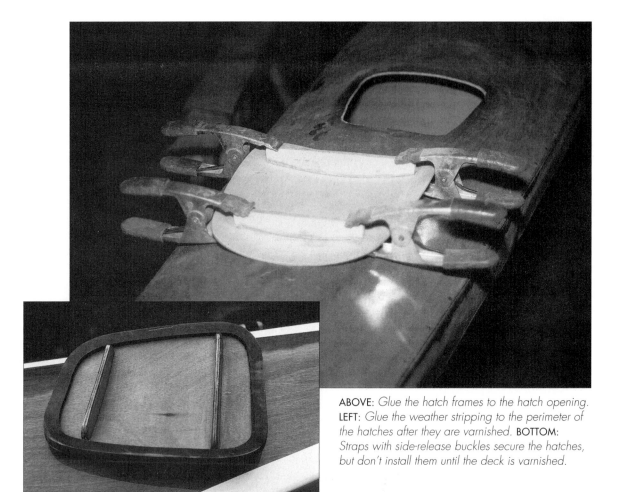

ABOVE: *Glue the hatch frames to the hatch opening.* LEFT: *Glue the weather stripping to the perimeter of the hatches after they are varnished.* **BOTTOM:** *Straps with side-release buckles secure the hatches, but don't install them until the deck is varnished.*

heated over a flame. Screw the straps into the sheer clamp so that they lie on the hatch covers over the hatch frames. Finally, attach the buckles to the straps.

Another hatch design seen on wooden kayaks consists of a hatch cover the same size as the hatch cutout that rests on and seals to a frame glued to the underside of the deck. This type of hatch can be designed to fit perfectly flush with the deck, giving the kayak a very sleek appearance. Hatches of this type are often held closed by small swiveling latches and, in my experience, they leak like sieves.

Footbraces

Strong, properly positioned footbraces are essential to efficient paddling. Much of the force of paddling is, or should be, transmitted through the footbraces. Kayaks with rudders must have footbraces that slide or pivot to control the rudder. If more than one person will paddle your kayak, it should be fitted with adjustable footbraces to accommodate various leg lengths. Footbraces should be positioned under the ball of the foot, and they should allow the paddler's knees to lightly touch the deck. So it's wise to sit in the boat to mark the position of the footbraces prior to installing them.

The simplest footbrace is a block of wood glued to the inside of the kayak. This footbrace is light and cheap, but it cannot be adjusted to fit other paddlers, nor does it permit you to adjust your foot position, which can be a luxury on a long trip. I recommend installing adjustable footbraces in all kayaks. The aluminum and plastic Northwest Designs footbraces (often called Yakima footbraces) favored by whitewater kayakers are probably the strongest and best-made on the market. Keepers plastic footbraces are a less expensive alternative.

Footbraces are subject to enormous loads; it's not uncommon for paddlers to tear footbraces out of kayaks. These loads should be distributed by backing plates installed under the footbraces. Backing plates may be rectangles of 3 mm or 4 mm plywood a few inches wider and longer than the footbrace or a piece of fiberglass tape epoxied to the inside of the hull. Footbraces that have aluminum rails are difficult to glue properly. The surface of aluminum oxidizes quickly when exposed to air, but the bond between aluminum

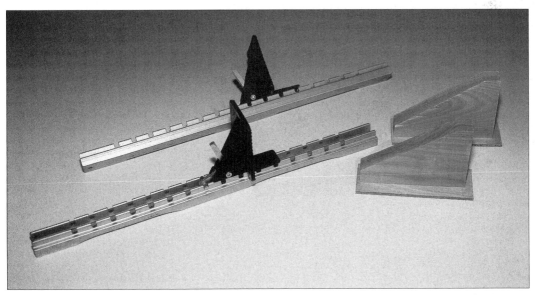

Commercially made adjustable footbraces should be installed in most boats. But simple wooden footbraces will do if only one paddler will use the boat.

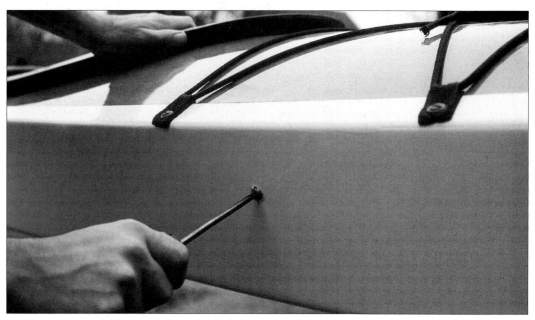

Footbraces are subject to great loads and should be secured by screws passing through the hull.

and epoxy is stronger if that surface is not oxidized. A way to increase the bond strength is to spread a little epoxy on the aluminum surface to be glued and then wet-sand it with a piece of coarse sandpaper. The epoxy will prevent air from reaching the freshly sanded surface. While the epoxy is still wet, screw the rail into place; be careful not to get any epoxy in the adjustment mechanism. 3M 5200 sealant can be used to install plastic footbraces. In addition to adhesive, footbraces must be through-bolted to the hull.

If you plan to install a rudder, you will need sliding footbraces, as described in the following chapter.

CHAPTER ELEVEN

Installing Rudders and Skegs

If you paddle in rough water, on windy days, or on long trips, or if you load your kayak with camping gear, you'll probably want to install a rudder or a retractable skeg on your new kayak. If, on the other hand, you do most of your paddling on calm, protected waters, there's little point in complicating a simple craft—and you can always add a rudder or skeg later.

Rudders

Rudders and rudder kits are available from many kayak shops and mail-order catalogs. Most are designed to be retrofitted to a specific plastic or fiberglass kayak, but with a little fiddling they can usually be adapted for use on a wooden kayak. I recommend Feathercraft rudders; they are the best-made and most reliable of any I've tried. The following instructions describe how to mount this specific brand, but most others are almost identical in function and appearance and can be installed in much the same manner. Likewise, the footbraces described are the Northwest Designs (Yakima) type mentioned in chapter 10.

Mounting the Rudder

Prior to installing the rudder, you must make an end-pour; that is, fill the end of the hull with epoxy to prevent water from

137

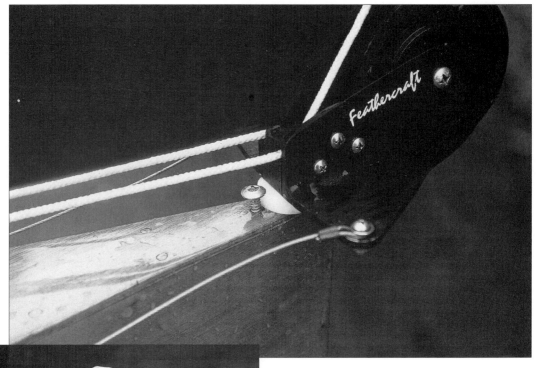

entering through the rudder pintle hole and to strengthen the mounting area. You may have done this when you built the boat; if not, see chapter 7. After the end-pour hardens, drill a ⅜-inch hole in the deck to accept the pintle. Hold the rudder beside the stern of the boat to judge the fore-and-aft position of the hole; the rudder must be able to swing past the stem. Be sure the mounting hole is vertical when the kayak is level. I find it easiest to stand behind the boat and aim the drill at the keel line. If you mount your rudder and find that the tip of the stern interferes with the swing of the rudder, plane a bit of wood off the stem and re-glass it. On kayaks with overhanging sterns, such as the Severn or my older Cape Charles and Tred Avon designs, you must actually cut 1 to 3 inches from the

TOP: *The rudder is mounted with the pintle in the end-pour. The screw prevents the rudder from falling out during rolls.* BOTTOM: *The hole for the rudder pintle should be perfectly vertical.*

end of the hull with a handsaw to allow the rudder to swing.

Next, seal the exposed plywood at the top edge of the mounting hole with epoxy. Rub a little waterproof grease on the pintle and mount the rudder. You do not need to install a metal bushing around the pintle. The epoxy end-pour is an excellent bearing surface that will last forever if you grease the pintle once or twice a year.

Finally, fit a retaining screw just forward of the white plastic disk that protrudes from the front of the rudder head, as shown opposite (top) and below (left). This screw's head holds down the rudder and prevents it from falling off during rolls or other capsizes. On some newer rudders a little plastic fitting is included that replaces the screw.

In *The Kayak Shop* I suggested selecting one of the rudder mounts made for various plastic and fiberglass boats and adapting it to fit on a wooden kayak. However, rudder mounts drag in the water, slowing the boat, they never seem to fit well, and a suitable one is difficult to find. Over the years I've found that the rudder-mounting method described above is superior, and it is the only method I've used for the past seven years.

Installing the Steering Cables

Mounting the rudder is only half the job; now you must run the steering cables, fit the rudder-lifting line, and install sliding

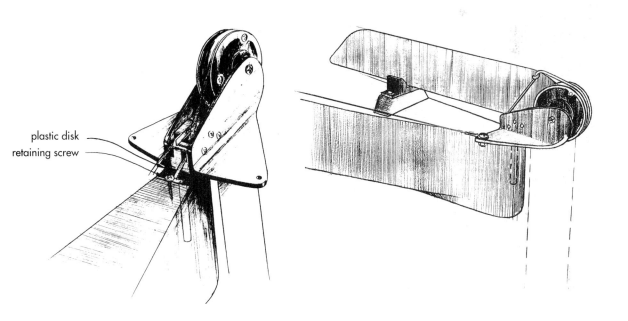

plastic disk

retaining screw

LEFT: *The disk and screw prevent the rudder from falling off when the boat is inverted.* **RIGHT:** *The rudder sits in the V-block when in the raised position.*

footbraces. The steering-cable housings will penetrate the deck about 2 feet forward of the rudder. These cables should bend as little as possible, so the points where the cables are attached to the rudder, penetrate the deck, and pass through the bulkhead should lie in a nearly straight line. Drill the holes through the deck at less than a 45-degree angle so that the cables won't bend sharply where they exit. Seal the cable housing to the deck and to the bulkhead with a dab of 3M 5200 sealant or with clear silicone caulk. Use plastic cable anchors to attach the cable housing to the deck just aft of the exit holes; this will prevent the cable from shifting and breaking the caulked seal. The screws for the cable anchors must

penetrate not only the deck but also the sheer clamps. Also, the cable housing should be attached to the sheer clamp in several places inside the kayak.

Thread the wire cables through the housing and attach them to the triangular rudder "wings" with the machine screws and locknuts. Loop the cables tightly over the screws and attach them with a swage. If possible, use a swaging tool to squeeze the swage shut; otherwise use a pair of Vise-Grips or a large pair of pliers. Squeeze tightly so that the cables won't come loose at a critical moment. Don't overtighten the screws, as the cables must pivot freely.

Installing Sliding Footbraces

Sliding footbraces are required to operate the rudder.

Footbraces for rudders must slide to control the rudder, so the adjustable footbraces described in chapter 10 must be fitted into a track, and then the track must be attached to the hull. You will still be able to adjust the footbraces by using the trigger mechanism behind the footpad to accommodate various leg lengths. Start by finding a comfortable position for the footbraces in your kayak. The footbraces are usually positioned 2 to 3 inches below the sheer and under the ball of the foot. Mark and drill the holes in the hull for the two machine screws that hold each black plastic track in place. Laminate two layers of fiberglass tape or plywood pads to the inside of hull to reinforce the area under the footbraces. Coat the outside of the plastic rail with 3M 5200 or another flexible sealant.

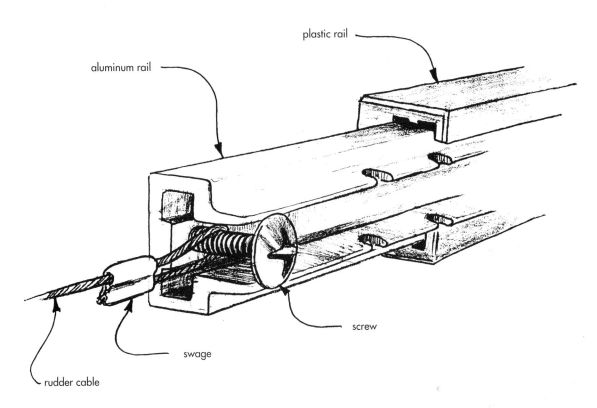

Attaching the steering cable to the sliding footbrace rail.

Dip the screw's threads into epoxy or sealant and screw the tracks into place. The nuts will jam into the recessed slot in the plastic rail. If the screws interfere with the sliding action of the footbraces, remove them and file or grind them down a bit.

Before attaching the cables, make sure that the footbraces are parallel when the rudder is centered and that the slots in the rails for clearing sand and mud face down. Loop the cables through a screw at the end of the aluminum rails or through the hole in the rail. Attach them with a swage.

Rigging the Lifting Line

The rudder is lifted out of the water by means of a loop of line (shown in the in the top photos on pages 138 and 142) led to within the paddler's reach. Pulling on one side of the loop raises the rudder, and pulling on the other side lowers it. A section of elastic cord attached to a plastic clip holds the loop taut, preventing it from loosening and tightening as the rudder swings. Rig the loop to pass through the clip just behind the paddler as well as through two cable anchors

installed on most rudders is long enough for most kayaks, but if you're installing the rudder on a very long single, you might need to substitute a longer lifting line to bring it within reach of the cockpit.

Mount the V-block as shown in the sketch on page 139 and the photo at left. Glue the wooden V-block mount to the deck to raise the V-block to the proper height for your kayak. A wooden V-block, rather than a commercially made plastic block, is a nice touch.

TOP: *The line for lifting and lowering the rudder is led to within reach of the paddler.* BOTTOM: *A custom V-block adds a nice touch to this kayak.*

Skegs

Skegs are small fins installed under the stern to improve tracking. They may be fixed, or they may retract like the centerboard on a sailboat. Fixed skegs can be made from aluminum plate or from thick

along the gunwale. These can be attached using the same screws that hold the hatch-cover straps and tie-downs. The lifting line

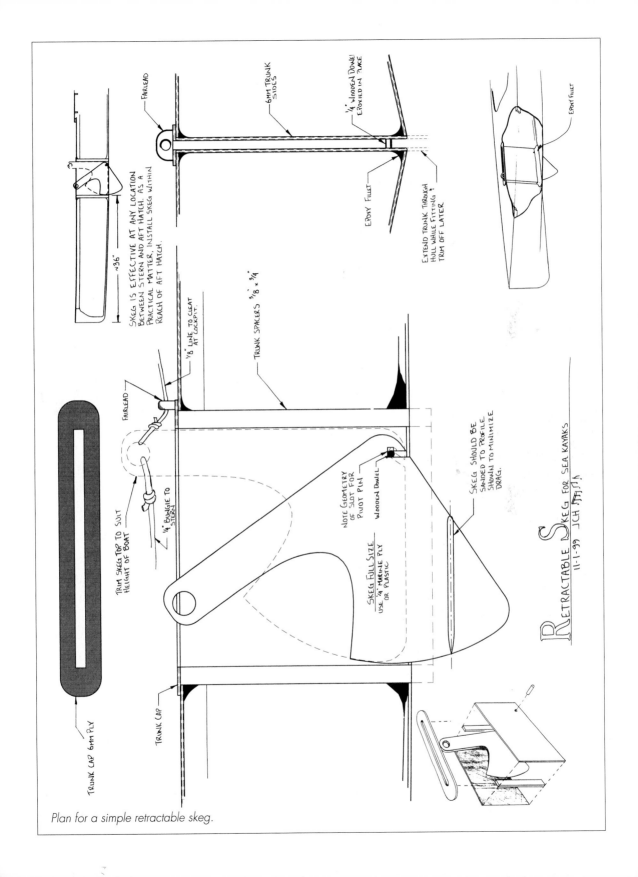

Plan for a simple retractable skeg.

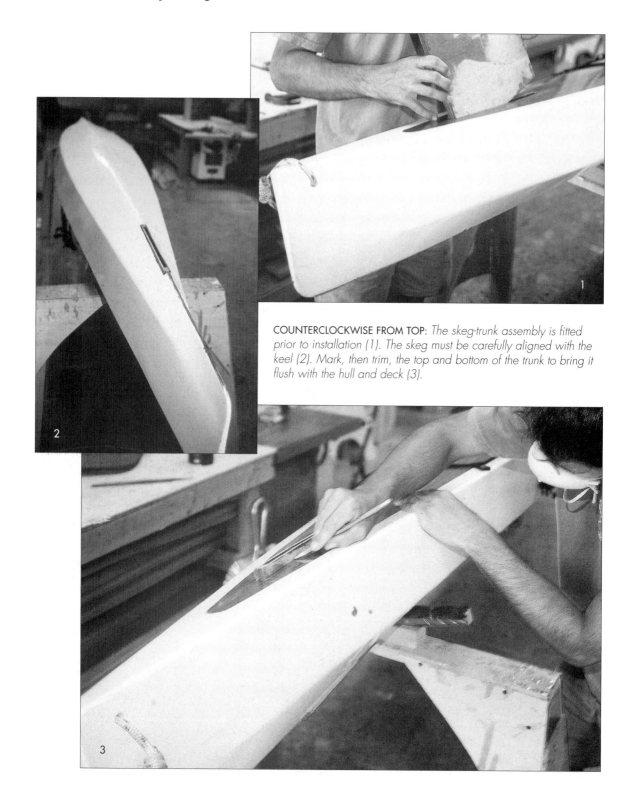

COUNTERCLOCKWISE FROM TOP: *The skeg-trunk assembly is fitted prior to installation (1). The skeg must be carefully aligned with the keel (2). Mark, then trim, the top and bottom of the trunk to bring it flush with the hull and deck (3).*

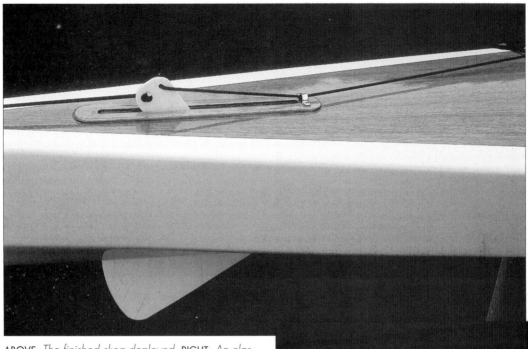

ABOVE: *The finished skeg deployed.* RIGHT: *An elastic cord keeps the skeg deployed unless the paddler tensions the lift line.*

plywood affixed to the hull with glue and/or fiberglass tape. If plywood is used for the skeg, it should also be reinforced with fiberglass along its bottom. Should you design a boat that does not hold course well, you may be able to "save" it by adding a small fixed skeg.

Some paddlers prefer retractable skegs to rudders; they seem to be particularly popular on English boats. Retractable skegs are used to improve a kayak's balance without the complications of a rudder. Of course, all they do is improve tracking; they can't really steer a boat.

The plan reproduced on page 143 shows a simple skeg that's easy to fit to any kayak. The skeg box, or *trunk*, is made from 6 mm plywood; the skeg itself can be

The skeg lift line is secured in a clam cleat near the cockpit.

cut from plywood, aluminum, or stiff plastic. An elastic cord holds the skeg in the down position, while a line led to the cockpit raises it. Notice that the skeg simply slips over a pivot pin, so it can easily be replaced if it is damaged or removed to clean out sand or seaweed trapped in the trunk. When installing a skeg, be certain that it is aligned with the keel. The last thing you want is a permanently mounted rudder that's always a few degrees off. Chesapeake Light Craft sells these skegs as kits that may be retrofitted to a wooden or fiberglass kayak.

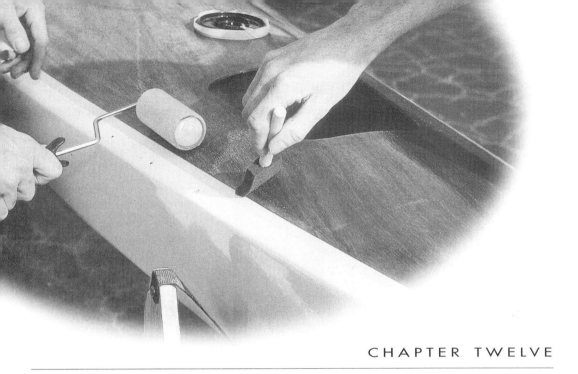

CHAPTER TWELVE

Finishing

I'd succeeded in laying on five flawless coats of varnish. The kayak I was working on was to be displayed at a large outdoor-equipment store to promote my seminar on kayak building. After painstakingly brushing on the sixth and final coat, I tiptoed out of the shop and locked the door. The next morning, ready to deliver my flawless new boat to the store, I opened the door to find that a squirrel had gotten into the shop and walked over my wet varnish.

The moral of this story is when you try to achieve a fine finish the deck is stacked against you. You'll struggle against bubbles, runs, dust, kamikaze insects, and squirrels. But it's worth the trouble: nothing shows the beauty of a wooden boat like six coats of varnish. Unfortunately, it's tempting to rush through this stage of construction, telling yourself that you only wanted a functional boat. Before you do, consider how much effort you've already put into the project.

Epoxy Saturation

Prior to varnishing or painting your kayak, coat the deck, coaming, and any other bare wood parts with epoxy. The epoxy soaks into the wood, filling and reinforcing the grain, particularly the grain opened by bending, as on the deck. It adds a tough outer skin that increases the hull's strength and resistance to abrasion,

147

Seal all wood surfaces with epoxy before applying the finish.

and it provides a smooth clear base that adds depth to the final finish. Epoxy also makes an ideal base for paint or varnish, finishes that usually fail when water finds its way into the wood and causes the paint or varnish to blister or lift. But epoxy bonds to the wood, making a waterproof shell that prevents water from undermining the finish.

As you know by now, epoxy doesn't flow or level well, so applying a smooth coat is difficult. Again, the best tool for applying epoxy is a foam roller. Roll a thin layer of epoxy over the entire surface; most of this first coat will be absorbed into the wood. Rollers tend to leave small bubbles on the epoxy's surface. These can be *tipped off* by running a disposable foam or

bristle brush over the fresh epoxy; just skim the surface with the tip of the brush to pop the bubbles. Brush out any runs or drips, or you'll have to sand them out later. When the epoxy has hardened, sand the surface lightly and then roll on the second coat of epoxy, again brushing out any bubbles and runs. Be particularly careful to seal exposed plywood edges, such as the underside of the coaming; if water enters the plywood's core, it can cause problems later.

Apply the sealing coat of epoxy when the air temperature is steady or falling. If you apply the coat early on a cool morning, the rising air temperature will cause the air in the wood to expand and escape through the wet epoxy. This is called *out-*

gassing; it causes thousands of tiny bubbles to form in the epoxy, which you'll have to sand smooth.

Sanding

No matter how carefully you roll, brush, or squeegee the epoxy onto your hull and deck, it won't be perfectly smooth. And even if the surface is perfect, varnish or paint won't adhere to shiny, unsanded epoxy. So resign yourself to at least a few more hours of sanding.

Before you start sanding, wash the boat with detergent and water to remove any amine blush left by the curing epoxy. Amine blush clogs sandpaper and prevents paint and varnish from drying. Two thorough washes with a scrub pad and warm, soapy water followed by a rinse will remove it. Sanding won't remove amine blush, but will only smear it around. If you used an epoxy that is resistant to blushing, such as MAS with slow hardener, you may skip this step.

Sanding is the least enjoyable part of building a boat, so try to make it as easy as possible. Wear a good-quality mask or respirator that will stop dust yet permit comfortable breathing, get a set of earplugs, and stock up on sandpaper so you're not sanding with worn-out sheets. Finally, consider sanding your boat outside on a breezy day.

Start with 80-grit paper on your random-orbital sander. Hold the sander flat against the hull; using the edge of the spinning disc or pad will make grooves that are difficult to smooth out. Work

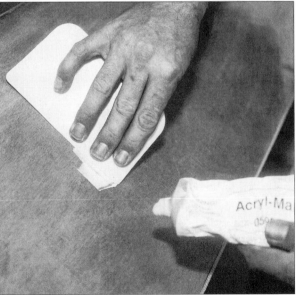

TOP: *Sanding, and lots of it, is the key to a good finish.*
BOTTOM: *Acrylic putty and high-build primer are used to fill low spots prior to painting.*

steadily from one end of the boat to the other. Change the sandpaper often, every 3 feet or so; fresh sandpaper cuts much faster and leaves fewer swirl marks. Do *not* use an electric sander on the chines, keel, stems, hull-to-deck joint, and other sharp edges—the sander will cut right through the epoxy and fiberglass on these joints. Even boatbuilders who have sanded dozens of hulls don't use a sander on sharp corners. Sand these areas by hand.

When you've finished sanding, the entire surface should be an even, dull white. Shiny spots indicate low or unsanded areas. If you accidentally sand through the epoxy layer—and you probably will—recoat the area and sand it again later. Next, you must sand the whole boat again, first using 120- and then 220-grit sandpaper to eliminate swirls and sanding marks. This won't take nearly as long as the initial sanding. Sand tricky areas, such as the coaming, by hand with 120- and 220-grit paper.

When you've finished the final sanding, take a break; then examine the entire surface of your boat inch by inch and circle every imperfection with a soft pencil. You'll be surprised at how many you find. Fill low spots with acrylic putty or with a fairing putty made by mixing epoxy with a lightweight, easily sanded thickener such as microballoons. You can use wood flour with epoxy for fairing instead, but it's harder to sand. Acrylic putty is available at all auto-parts stores and many marine stores. It is a fast-drying paste that sands easily, but it shrinks as it dries and so is only suitable for very shallow imperfections. Of course, you'll use fairing com-

pound or putty only under paint, not under varnish.

Some builders like to roll on several more coats of epoxy after the initial sanding to build up a deep, glasslike base for the varnish. These subsequent coats must be sanded too. I've done this on a few kayaks and the resulting finish is very impressive, but it sure takes a lot of work and it adds a lot of extra weight to the boat.

After sanding, wash your kayak again to remove all traces of sanding dust. Epoxy dust is tenacious stuff that won't just rinse off with a casual spray. You'll need to go over the boat several times with a wet towel or sponge.

Primer

If a show-quality paint job is your goal, use a high-build primer under the paint. This is a thick, easily sanded primer that fills even the tiniest imperfections in the hull. Roll on two coats and allow them to dry, then sand off most of what you've applied. This will fill the low spots and scratches, leaving a perfectly smooth surface. Sanding high-build primer generates copious quantities of baby powder–like dust, so sand it outside. Because most primers are a bit softer than epoxy and the paint that goes over them, primed hulls may tend to dent or scratch more readily than unprimed hulls. Some high-build primers use talc as filler, while others use microballoons, which are a bit more durable. I know a boatbuilder who makes his own primer by mixing filler into thinned paint; his finishes are very impressive and fairly durable.

Finishes

You must apply some finish to your boat. A few coats of epoxy may look like varnish, but epoxy deteriorates in sunlight, turning milky and dull. It needs to be protected from ultraviolet (UV) radiation with either paint or marine varnish. Most builders will want to finish their hull, deck, and interior bright. You'll also need to varnish inside your kayak since sunlight strikes there too. There is, however, an argument to be made for painting the hull. Paint holds up better than varnish, is more resistant to abrasion and easier to touch up, requires fewer coats, and you can use fairing compound and high-build primer under the paint to achieve a smoother, more efficient, and faster finish. Even larger scratches or chips in the wood can be repaired with thickened epoxy and hidden under paint. Surprisingly, however, surface irregularities and poor sanding seem more noticeable on a painted surface than on a varnished one. I think this is because people tend to be awestruck by shiny expanses of varnished wood and don't notice the surface details under it. Also, the pattern of the grain acts like camouflage, hiding shapes and details. One last point: you can always paint over the varnish later, but there isn't much hope of varnishing over the paint.

CHOOSING VARNISH AND PAINT

You'll probably choose to varnish at least part of your kayak. Use only high-quality marine varnish. Marine varnishes have UV filters that allow them to stand up to sunlight longer than other types, and UV radiation is what eventually causes varnish, as well as epoxy, to break down. Stick to established marine brands, such as Z-Spar, Epifanes, and Interlux. Varnishing isn't easy; don't make it tougher by using an inferior household varnish or a one-part polyurethane varnish. So-called spar varnishes, sold at home-improvement and hardware stores, are not acceptable. Nor are one-part marine polyurethane varnishes and finishes, tung-oil furniture finishes, various concoctions intended for use on exterior teak, and so on.

Each of the marine finish manufacturers makes several types of varnish. There are subtle differences between the types as well as the brands. Much of varnishing involves getting a feel for the varnish you're using, so don't change brands or types once you've gotten the hang of using one. Chesapeake Light Craft uses Z-Spar's Captain's Varnish exclusively. I know that Z-Spar makes a high-end varnish called Flagship, but we've found that it is harder to apply than Captain's Varnish, so that's what we've stuck with for 8 years.

Two-part polyurethane marine varnishes are another option. They are very hard and very resistant to abrasion, stand up well to sunlight, and are compatible with epoxy. Despite these advantages, I still prefer traditional oil-based varnishes. I've tried two-part polyurethane varnishes, but I'm still undecided about them because they're very expensive, harder to apply than oil-based varnishes, and relatively untested. In addition, I like the golden color of oil-based varnishes and the warm glow they impart to mahogany; in general, two-part polyurethanes are perfectly clear. This type of varnish is essentially a clear paint, so if you choose to use it, follow the instructions for applying two-part polyurethane paint.

I should mention that water-based varnishes are getting better all the time, but I have not found one whose performance approaches that of traditional tung oil–based varnish. The types I've experimented with are not as transparent and do not hold up as well as real varnish, and they lack the latter's gold tone. When choosing varnishes, don't believe advertising claims—pick well-established products used by professionals.

There are several options in choosing paint, but most builders will use marine enamel, one-part polyurethane, or two-part polyurethane. Marine enamels are the traditional oil-based paints. They give a hard finish that's slightly flat rather than glossy. Enamels are not expensive, as marine paints go, and they are available in many colors. On the down side, some types don't dry well over epoxy. Many builders prefer the one-part polyurethanes to traditional enamels because they are harder and glossier, but I like the slightly dull, old-fashioned look.

One-part marine polyurethanes, such as Interlux's popular Brightside paint, are the choice of most kayak builders, and for good reason. They are almost as glossy and durable as the two-part variety but far easier to apply. And they are available in a wide range of colors from several manufacturers. If you carefully apply them with a foam roller, most people will assume that a professional sprayed your finish.

Two-part polyurethane is harder and glossier than the one-part variety. In fact, fiberglass boat manufacturers have been known to paint their show boats with it because it's so much glossier than gelcoat. Unfortunately, two-part polyurethane is also far more expensive and far more difficult to apply. The extreme gloss and relative thinness of this paint bring out every flaw in the underlying surface, so you must prepare your hull with fanatical care. If you do decide to try a two-part polyurethane, be sure to also buy the special thinner that is required to bring it to a brushable consistency.

There are numerous types of paint on the market, and new ones are being introduced continually. In *The Kayak Shop* I recommended exterior house paint for a quick-and-dirty finish. Today there are several industrial latex paints intended for outdoor machinery and other metal surfaces that are as easy to apply but more durable than house paint. I tried one of these on the interior of my rowboat a few years ago, and it has held up remarkably well. A professional paint shop will carry these products and its staff will be able to explain how to apply them. And most paint companies have technical representatives who will happily discuss the merits and applications of their various products with you.

In choosing the color of your paint, consider whether you'll be able to get more of it when you need to touch up a scrape. White paint is always available; "minty teal" will (hopefully) be discontinued soon. Some less popular colors are only manufactured once or twice a year, so if you run out, you might not get more for many months. Actually, there are several reasons to choose a white hull: kayaks painted a light color are cooler in the sun; many paddlers think that light-colored hulls look better with a varnished deck; scratches don't show up as much on a white hull; and white is visible from a distance. On the other hand, many sea-kayaking pundits point out that a yellow, orange, or red hull would be easiest to spot in an emergency.

You may need to thin any paint or varnish slightly if you are working on a hot day, but never by more than 10 percent. Buy the thinner recommended by the manufacturer. I know that you suspect that you're paying $15 for a few ounces of mineral spirits, but the recommended thinners always seem to work better.

Varnishing just the deck of the kayak will require close to a quart of varnish. The hull and the deck can be done with two quarts of varnish. Painting the hull of a kayak will use up the better part of a quart of paint and, if you choose to use it, a full quart of primer.

Tools for Finishing

Professionals apply finishes either with cheap, disposable foam brushes and rollers or with very expensive, top-quality badger bristle brushes—they don't use anything in between. I recommend sticking to disposable foam brushes and rollers; not only are they cheaper but you don't have to clean them. If you object to using disposable brushes for environmental reasons,

think about how much brush cleaner you'd use to clean a badger bristle brush in the course of painting your kayak. (Consider also the effect on those denuded badgers.) The large, relatively flat surfaces of a kayak are difficult to coat with a brush, so you might consider using a foam roller to apply the finish. It's a little tricky using a roller with varnish, but once you get the hang of it, it's very fast and effective.

Buy 2-inch foam brushes; try to find the sort with wooden, not plastic, handles

Mask off painted areas with 3M Fine Line tape; don't use paper masking tape.

as they seem to last longer. Use foam rollers of the type made for use with lacquer or epoxy. These are usually yellow with a very short nap, ¼ inch or so. Do not buy the black general-purpose foam rollers that disintegrate when used with epoxy. Cut 7- or 9-inch rollers in half and use them with half-width roller frames.

You can also apply paint and varnish with a spray gun, but it requires special skills that most of us don't have. If you decide to spray, contact the manufacturer for specific instructions. Some marine finishes are extremely toxic when atomized, and a positive-pressure respirator must be worn while spraying them.

If applying both paint and varnish to the same boat, you will need to mask one part while you apply finish to the other. Use only the plastic 3M Fine Line masking tape available at auto-parts and marine stores. Marine finishes are thin and will bleed under regular paper masking tape. The trick to getting a nice clean delineation between paint and varnish is to press the edge of the tape down firmly so paint can't seep under it. Don't leave masking tape in place for more than a couple of days, or it may take you a couple more days to remove it.

Dust Is the Enemy

The single most important step you can take toward ensuring a nice paint or varnish finish is to work in a dust-free area. Woodworking being anything but dust-free, try to find a room other than your shop in which to paint and varnish. If possible, wet down the floor to settle dust stirred up by walking, vacuum the room, and keep the doors and windows closed to minimize air movement after you've finished. Also, change out of the clothes you wore when sanding and rinse the dust out of your hair and off your arms. I've heard several reports of perfectionists who varnish naked.

If you see tiny "bubbles" in your dry varnish, they are dust particles. Yes, I know they look like bubbles, but they are dust. And I do believe that you vacuumed and cleaned and wet down the floor and varnished naked (much to the neighbor's consternation, no doubt), but those bubbles are still dust. Unless you have a special paint room or clean room, there will be some dust in your finish. All you can hope to do is minimize it.

Applying Varnish and Paint

Prior to applying paint or varnish, read the directions on the can. No one knows more about a paint or varnish than its manufacturer, and their advice is free and right there in front of you. Most paint manufacturers also give out free literature full of tips on applying their products; Interlux even includes a how-to audiotape with one of its paints. You'll notice that much of the instructions are devoted to preparing the surface prior to painting. You've probably heard this before, but it's important enough to repeat: preparation really is 90 percent of a good finish job.

Varnish and paint are sensitive to temperature and humidity. If possible,

varnish or paint only on warm, dry days. If you're working outdoors, put the finish on early so it will be almost dry before dew starts to form in the evening. Avoid painting or varnishing outdoors on very hot days, on cold days, in direct sunlight, on windy days, or when there are lots of bugs around. Lastly, if there's any chance of rain, don't varnish outdoors; if it's already raining, don't even varnish indoors.

Never use varnish or paint directly out of the can; instead, pour as much as you'll need for one coat into a clean paper cup or can. And when you finish, don't even think of pouring the remainder back into the can. If you'll be using a foam roller, pour the paint or varnish into a clean roller tray.

At Chesapeake Light Craft varnish is usually applied with a 2-inch foam brush.

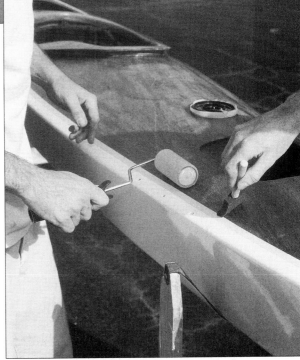

TOP: *When using foam brushes to apply varnish, lay the varnish on across the grain, then smooth it out in the direction of the grain.* BOTTOM: *Rolling and tipping varnish or paint is easier if you have a helper.*

Wet-sand between coats to level and dull the surface.

There is a technique to applying varnish so that it's smooth, glossy, and free of runs. Dip just the tip of the brush into the varnish; don't overload it. Lay on a thin coat by brushing across the grain. Smooth, or tip, the varnish by brushing it in the direction of the grain; use slow, deliberate brush strokes. Start a foot or so from the bow and varnish toward the tip of the bow. Dip the brush again and start a foot further back. Lay on the varnish again; then brush it with the grain, ending each brush stroke in the wet area you just finished. Continue varnishing in this way. If you look back at your work and see a few dry spots, don't be concerned, you'll repair them on the next coat. But runs are a cause for concern—they indicate that the coat is too thick. Learning to brush paint and varnish takes practice.

Don't be disappointed if the first coat is less than perfect. By the fourth or fifth coat you'll be an expert.

Of course, you could apply paint with a brush just as you did the varnish, but I recommend applying paint with a foam roller, then tipping it out with a brush. (This technique works well for varnish, too, if the varnish is thinned a little.) When using a roller, don't overload it with paint or varnish. Try to lay on a thin, even coat over about 1 square foot of the surface. Immediately put down the roller, pick up your brush, and gently run it over the surface to pop bubbles left by the roller and to smooth any runs. The brush should just skim the paint. It's easier to have an assistant tip the paint as you continue to apply it.

Paint sets up quickly; you'll need to work quickly so that you're always rolling into a wet edge rather than into paint or varnish that has started to set. When you're finished, check for squirrels and lock your shop.

It's best to wait two days after applying the first coat of paint or varnish to recoat, then wait overnight between subsequent coats. Hand-sand lightly between coats with 400-grit wet/dry paper. In case you're not familiar with wet/dry sandpaper, use it on a rubber sanding block just as you would ordinary sandpaper, but dip the block and paper into a bucket of water every few minutes. The water washes away the dust that would otherwise quickly clog such fine sandpaper. Remember that your aim is to dull and smooth the surface, not to remove all the finish you so carefully applied the day before. Sanding the surface should take only a few minutes. Wipe off the sanding dust with wet paper towels and then with a tack cloth.

You'll need at least four coats of varnish for a good finish, six or seven for a yacht-quality finish, and after ten coats, even your most jaded plastic-boat-paddling friends will want wooden kayaks. Marine paints are thin and you'll probably need at least three coats, but some colors, yellow in particular, require five or six.

Finally, don't be discouraged if your first coat of paint or varnish looks awful. You can sand it smooth and start over on the next coat. You have until the fourth or fifth coat to get the hang of it.

CHAPTER THIRTEEN

Fitting Out

Your kayak is almost finished. Before you paddle off into the sunset, take a few hours to see to the details that make paddling safer, more convenient, and more comfortable. These may include deck grab handles, deck tie-downs, a bilge pump, a compass, cockpit padding, and perhaps a rudder or skeg. You'll also need a paddle, so I'll describe two that are easy to make and pleasant to use.

Bow and Stern Handles

Grab handles at the bow and stern are an important safety feature that should be installed on every kayak. Grab handles allow you to easily hang on to a kayak when per-

Strong grab handles are essential for safety and convenience.

159

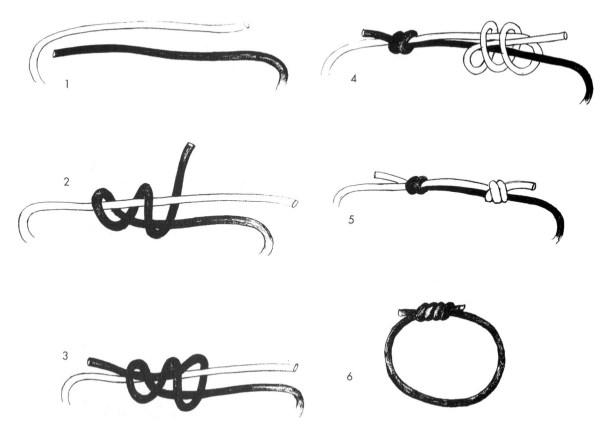

The proper knots for grab handles and deck elastics.

forming a rescue, when you wet-exit, or if the kayak is to be towed. They also provide a way to tie the boat when transporting it on a car rack, an attachment point for a painter so the kayak can be tied to a dock, and a convenient means for two people to carry it. The grab handles must be strong and securely attached to the boat; consider how much force is put on them when you manhandle a fully loaded or flooded kayak.

The simplest way to install grab handles is to drill holes a few inches from the tips of the bow and stern and then pass loops of line through them. It's easier to do this before finishing the boat. Of course, you'll need to make end-pours prior to drilling these holes.

Good grab handles can also be made by screwing lengths of tubular nylon webbing to the deck and sheer clamp. Tubular tape is softer and easier on your hands than the flat straps you'll use to hold down hatches. Attach the grab handles, which should be 6 to 8 inches long, with 1-inch #10 screws and finish washers. Seal these, and all screw holes, with epoxy or silicone caulk.

Another method of attaching grab handles is to use padeyes. The grab loops and painter can simply be tied through these. Padeyes are available in bronze or stainless steel and look better on a more traditional boat than on a sleek, modern sea kayak. The padeyes should be of the heavy-duty type that use four screws rather than just two. All four screws must bite into the sheer clamps or end-pour; otherwise they will eventually pull out.

Deck Rigging

Most paddlers find it convenient to carry some gear on deck. The most common tie-down system consists of several elastic cords crisscrossed across the deck. Though most kayak manufacturers run the elastic cord through plastic or metal eyelets or through fancy recessed fittings glassed into

TOP: *Another way to install grab handles.* MIDDLE: *Padeyes should be secured with four screws that penetrate the sheer clamps or the end-pour.* BOTTOM: *A shock-cord fitting made from a loop of 1-inch webbing.*

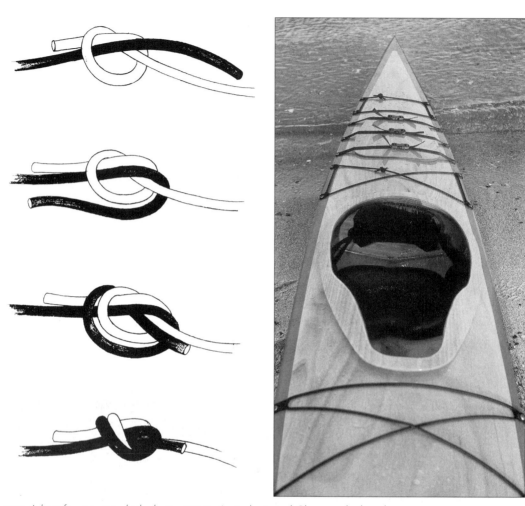

LEFT: *A knot for securing deck elastic.* RIGHT: *A nicely rigged Chesapeake kayak.*

the deck, I prefer to run it through loops of nylon webbing screwed to the sheer clamps. This method makes low-profile attachments that don't trap water or snag gear or clothes during a wet reentry and weigh less than recessed fittings.

Be sure that the eyelets or nylon-webbing loops you use are screwed into the sheer clamps and not just into the deck. If you use nylon loops, add a finish washer over the webbing to prevent it

from pulling off the screwhead. I normally use ¼-inch elastic cord for deck tie-downs; it's a little thicker than the cord used on some kayaks, but it holds the gear more securely and costs only a few cents more.

Before rigging your boat, think about what will be carried on deck. It may be fashionable to run a spiderweb of elastic cord over your boat, but most of this will go unused. Loading gear on deck is detrimental to stability and adds windage, so you'll want to limit what you carry there to a few items. Most paddlers carry a chart, a water bottle, and perhaps a waterproof camera or a small dry bag under the deck elastics. An X-shaped pattern of elastic just ahead of and behind the cockpit will suffice for most gear. Another loop behind the aft hatch will hold a spare paddle. And the elastic behind the cockpit will secure the paddle during reentries. I see no need to add more elastic cord; even when carrying fishing gear this arrangement has proven sufficient.

Many paddlers install perimeter grab lines around the boat. If you find yourself swimming in rough water, these make it easier to grab your kayak before it blows away. Grab lines should be of ¼-inch Dacron line and may be secured using many of the same webbing loops or eyelets that are used for securing the elastic deck tie-downs. You might also want to rig a towline and install a small plastic cleat to secure it.

Compasses, Bilge Pumps, and Other Deck-Mounted Gear

One of the great things about having a wooden boat is that it's easy to customize. Compasses, bilge pumps, fishing-rod holders, water-bottle holders, or most anything else you can think of can be mounted on deck. In most cases all you need to do is glue a backing plate under the deck and screw your new toy to it.

A wooden compass mount adds a nice touch.

Though in some parts of the world paddlers see little need for a compass, those of us who paddle in Maine, for example, know that fog can be more common than sunshine for many weeks of the year. And only a fool would set off for a long paddle without a chart and compass. In *The Kayak Shop* I suggested installing the compass on a spare forward hatch cover so it could be removed. Today several compasses are available that snap off their bases; I recommend buying one of these if you live in a place where theft is a problem. Don't mount the compass too close to the cockpit. It should be far enough forward so that you can see it over gear stowed under the forward tie-downs. And your eyes should not continually refocus as they do when you try to read a compass that's too close to the cockpit.

A bilge pump is another vital safety feature on a sea kayak. You can carry a handheld pump in the cockpit or under the deck tie-downs, or you might mount a diaphragm pump on deck. If you decide to install a deck-mounted pump, position it near the aft deck beam or bulkhead and glue a generously sized backing plate under the deck. You can exert substantial pressure on the deck when operating a diaphragm-type pump. Foot-operated bilge pumps are becoming more popular; they are easy to install on wooden kayaks, though it's far easier to install them prior to attaching the deck. Although foot-operated pumps have a lower capacity than deck-mounted or handheld pumps, I feel they add a degree of safety over other types. The foot-operated pump can be used while you continue to paddle and

brace, which is important because pumps are most often required in rough conditions when both your hands are best kept on the paddle. Foot-operated pumps are available from many kayak shops. Some paddlers adapt foot-operated galley pumps meant for larger sail and powerboats for this purpose; these are available at marine-supply stores.

Seats

Finding a comfortable seat is essential to enjoying your new boat. Because our anatomies differ—both in shape and in the amount of natural padding—the seat that one paddler finds luxurious another will find torturous. The degree of comfort required depends on the time you spend in your boat. We can make do with a marginal seat for a few hours, but on a long trip that same arrangement would be untenable. Here are several options for seats; I hope one of them will agree with you.

A simple yet comfortable seat can be made from two layers of ¾-inch closed-cell foam using the pattern shown opposite. Cut the bottom ring and the seat top with a saber saw, bandsaw, or keyhole saw. Sand the edges with coarse sandpaper and round over the top edge. Glue the two layers together with waterproof contact cement. The best cement for gluing foam is the sort used to attach automotive weather stripping, available at auto-parts stores. Glue the outside edges of the seat into the boat, leaving the area along the keel loose so water can drain under it.

Not all types of foam are appropriate

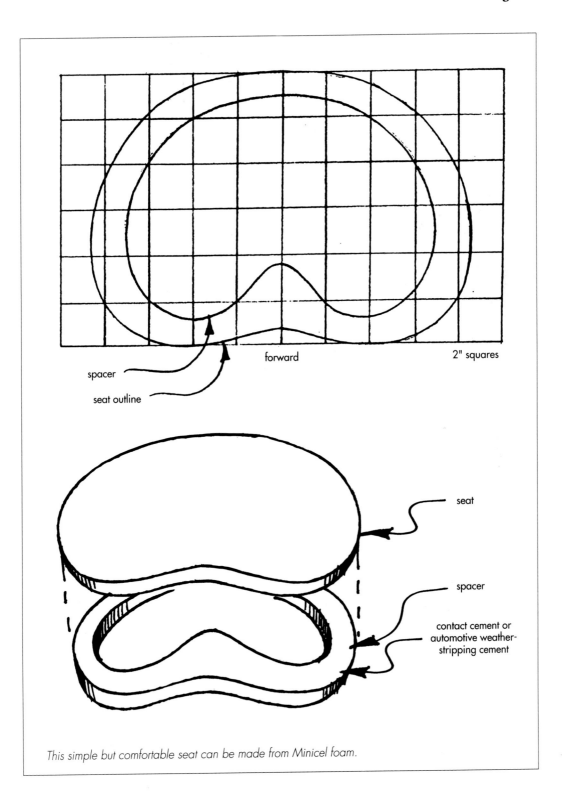

spacer

seat outline

forward

2" squares

seat

spacer

contact cement or automotive weather-stripping cement

This simple but comfortable seat can be made from Minicel foam.

for seats and cockpit padding. Many types, such as Ensolite, which is used for sleeping-bag pads, lose their memory and become hard and uncomfortable rather quickly. Minicel foam, which is available at many kayak shops, is a closed-cell foam that keeps its shape and does not seem to absorb any water. Ethafoam is another possible choice, though it's not as attractive as Minicel. It can absorb some water, and it is difficult to find in small sheets.

Another option is to carve a seat from a solid block of 3-inch-thick Minicel foam using a sander or grinder fitted with the coarsest sandpaper available. In two or three hours you can sand out a "scoop" that fits your posterior exactly. I can, from experience, tell you that you probably won't get it right the first time.

Though it is possible to make your own backrest, I usually install whitewater kayak–style backbands, such as the Rapid Pulse backband. Backbands are simple, lightweight, and easy to adjust. They provide sufficient support without giving the feeling that you're sitting in a chaise longue. Novice paddlers often lean back too far when paddling; if you find the backrest uncomfortable, you may simply be putting too much weight on it.

Several companies make aftermarket seats for fiberglass and wooden kayaks. When we evaluated aftermarket seats to sell at Chesapeake Light Craft, we sat in virtually every seat available, and selected the Creature Comfort seat and the Happy Bottom Pad as the most comfortable. The Happy Bottom Pad is a molded-foam seat,

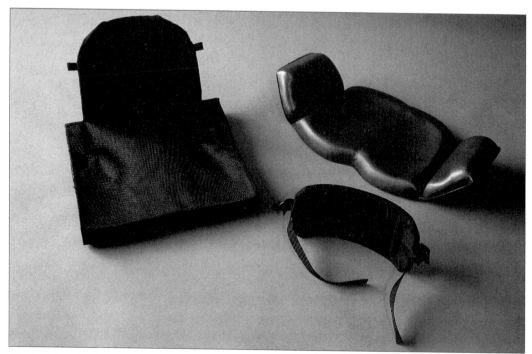

On the left is the Creature Comfort seat; on the right, a molded-foam Happy Bottom Pad; and below, a Rapid Pulse whitewater-style backband.

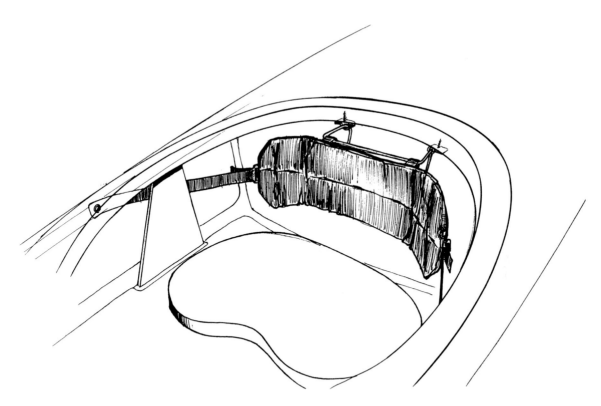

Installing a whitewater-style backband.

shaped much like a tractor seat, with attached hip braces; most paddlers find it quite comfortable. The Creature Comfort seat is my first choice for long trips. It has a bottom pad carved from a thick block of foam and covered with a mesh fabric that allows water to drain quickly. The attached padded backrest can be adjusted using a cord led to the sheer clamps.

Cockpit Padding

A solid, often repeated bit of advice is: one should not sit in a kayak, one should wear a kayak. To paddle efficiently, particularly in rough water, the paddler must be locked into the boat. Knees, hips, butt, and feet should be in contact with the kayak. When rolling or bracing, for example, it is the paddler's knee that "lifts" the boat. And it would not do to slide off the seat when leaning the kayak. This is why experienced paddlers spend considerable time getting their craft "padded out." Using thin sheets of Minicel foam, pad the hip braces and the area where your knees touch the deck. Some paddlers also like to add foam to the area under their thighs and heels. Again, use automotive weather-stripping cement to glue the foam.

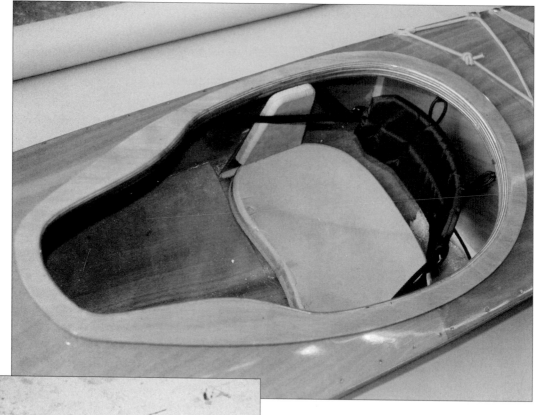

Paddles

The kayaker's paddle is a most personal piece of gear. There's a wide variety of paddle shapes, lengths, materials, and blade orientations from which to choose. This variety demonstrates that the human body is wonderfully adaptable, but it can make choosing a first paddle tough. I recommend that serious paddlers buy the best paddle they can afford. The spare paddle or a paddle for occasional use can be homemade; a plan and instructions for making two paddles are reproduced later in this chapter. Here's some information that will help in choosing a paddle.

Novice paddlers often ask why the

TOP: *This kayak has a comfortable, well-padded cockpit.*
BOTTOM: *Ferrules allow paddles to be assembled in right-hand-control, left-hand-control, and unfeathered geometry.*

blades on some paddles are set at right angles to each other. Called *feathered* paddles, they allow the blade that is out of the water to slice cleanly through the air. Some paddlers develop wrist or elbow pain from using a feathered paddle. Setting the blades at an angle of less than 90 degrees can minimize this, so in most modern feathered paddles the angle between the blades is 70 to 80 degrees. When using a feathered paddle, the grip of one hand is kept loose while the other rotates the paddle.

A paddle set so that the right hand rotates is called a *right-hand-control paddle*, while a paddle set so that the left hand rotates is referred to as a *left-hand-control paddle*. The front of the blade must be oriented in a specific way for right- or left-hand control; a right-hand-control paddle, for example, could not be used by a kayaker accustomed to left-hand control.

What kind of paddle should a novice choose? I recommend a *breakdown*, or two-piece, paddle with a ferrule that allows the paddle to be assembled in any of the three positions. Once you become accustomed to a particular blade orientation, stick with it. In an emergency you'll likely react as if the paddle is the type you learned with. If you're used to a feathered paddle and you try for quick brace with an unfeathered model, you may find that the blade has entered the water on edge and you are now attempting an Eskimo roll.

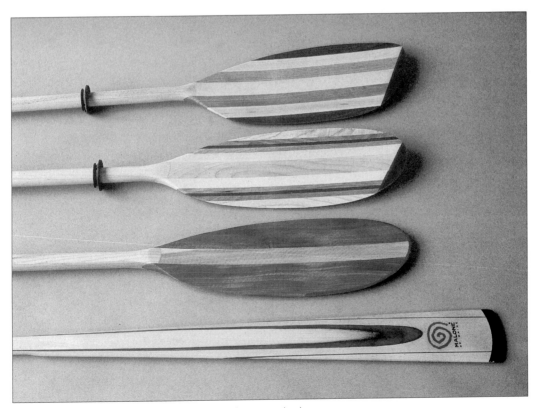

There are well-made wooden paddles to suit almost any budget.

Simple paddles made from the plans in this book.

Most modern blades are asymmetrical, or shaped to lessen twist as they enter and exit the water. Wider blades with more surface area are thought to provide more power than narrower, smaller blades, while the latter are said to be less tiring. But there is probably little difference as paddlers simply adjust their effort to compensate for blade size. Paddles with narrower blades are easier to use in strong winds.

Traditional *Greenland*- or *Inuit-style* paddles have long, narrow blades. They therefore require an entirely different technique than conventional, or western, paddles. Proponents of these paddles claim that they put less stress on the paddler's joints, make rolling and bracing easier, and behave better in high winds. In general, Greenland paddles are best suited to very narrow kayaks with low foredecks. The size and shape of a Greenland paddle should fit the paddler's anatomy perfectly; for this reason, many Greenland paddles are homemade. If you are interested in

making a Greenland paddle, I suggest getting a copy of paddle maker George Ellis's booklet *Paddlemaking 101*.

Until recently all paddles were made of wood, but today fiberglass paddles are also popular. Wooden paddles vary from the cheapest varieties, which are little more than wooden dowels with plywood blades, to laminated and carved masterpieces. The best of these have laminated shafts as well as laminated blades. Light woods such as cedar, bass, or spruce make up most of the paddle, while harder woods such as ash, oak, or walnut are used along the edge of the blade. Fiberglass paddles are also light, sometimes lighter than wood, and maintenance-free. In addition to normal fiberglass, lighter, but more expensive, versions are made with graphite. Some paddles are made with fiberglass shafts and plastic blades; these are a bit heavier than paddles made entirely of fiberglass, with the extra weight in the blades. I would buy a less expensive wooden paddle instead. Aluminum shafts are found only on the cheapest paddles and should be avoided by serious paddlers.

For maximum efficiency, the paddle should be just long enough so that the blade can be immersed without the paddle or fingers hitting the deck when the paddle is held in the normal position. If the paddle is too long, the effort of the blade will be applied further from the kayak, making the kayak turn. A relatively short paddle requires a higher stroke rate than some kayakers are comfortable with; it feels much like riding a bicycle in too low a gear. Lengthening the paddle gives the paddler more leverage, as does a higher gear on a bicycle, but the resulting lower cadence requires more pressure on each stroke to maintain the same speed. There are a number of factors to be considered when fitting a paddle. Paddlers who prefer an aggressive, racing technique and hold their paddles in a more vertical position require shorter paddles, while those who hold their paddles in a more leisurely, horizontal manner need longer paddles. Likewise, boats with higher decks or wider beams demand longer paddles. Generally, 220 cm to 230 cm paddles are about right for most single kayaks, and 240 cm to 250 cm paddles are good for wide singles and doubles.

Making Simple Paddles

High-quality kayak paddles are expensive but well worth buying. They are perfectly balanced, light, have efficient blade shapes, and are hard to equal. Nonetheless, some paddlers simply can't afford a high-end paddle, or they want a spare paddle or extra paddles for the kids or for friends. So here are two designs that are easy to make and work fairly well (see page 172).

These plans were originally drawn as full-size patterns so the builder could simply trace the shape onto the blade blank. Because they couldn't be reproduced here at full size, I've added some dimensions that you can use to make full-size drawings. Or you could take this book to a copy shop and have the plans reproduced at full size. (Don't try this with kayak plans; there will be far too much distortion.)

MAKING THE DIAMOND-BLADE PADDLE

The diamond-blade paddle is well suited to general touring and very simple to make. The paddle shaft is composed of two pieces of pine or spruce 1-inch half-round molding and a 1- by ¼-inch piece of lattice; these are available at most lumberyards. The lattice may be replaced with a strip of mahogany or other dark wood to provide an attractive contrasting stripe. The paddle blade is made of 6 mm marine-grade plywood.

Cut the two half-round moldings 22 inches shorter than the overall paddle length. Cut the lattice or spacer strip 48 inches shorter than the overall paddle length. With your block plane, taper the ends of the half-round molding as shown on the plans. Next, copy the blade's shape from the plans onto your plywood and cut the plywood to shape.

Coat the flat sides of the half-round molding with thickened epoxy and assemble the paddle as shown on the plans. Clamp the parts together and wipe up any epoxy that has squeezed out of the joints. After the epoxy has cured, sand the paddle and apply a coat of unthickened epoxy to the entire paddle. If you wish to make a breakdown paddle, it's a simple matter to cut the paddle in half and then fit a ferrule to reconnect it.

MAKING THE ASYMMETRICAL PADDLE

The asymmetrical paddle is designed to relieve the twisting or torque common to many wider paddles. It is a light, efficient paddle designed for touring or racing. It

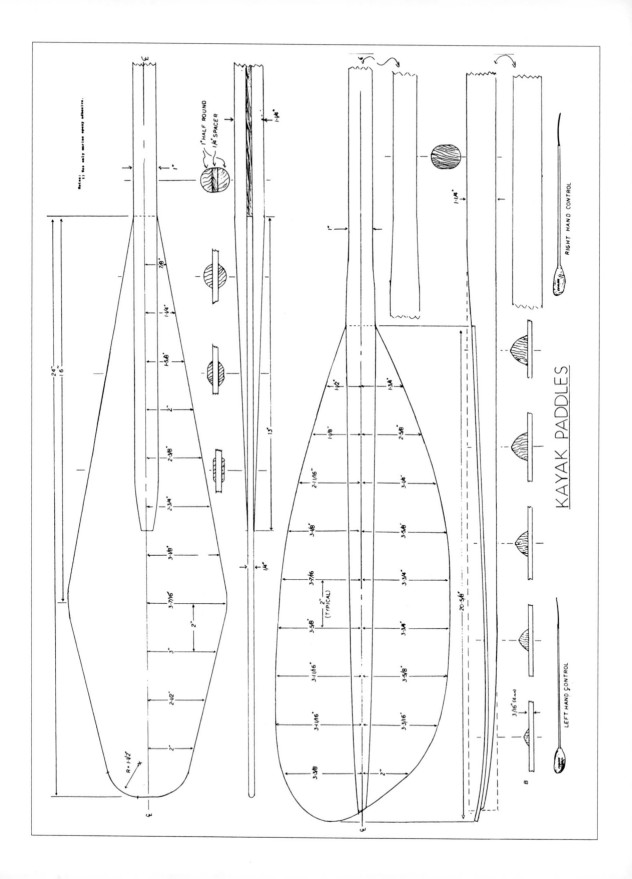

KAYAK PADDLES

may be built feathered or unfeathered, or a ferrule may be fitted so that it can be used either way. Because it involves more carving, this paddle is a bit more difficult to make than the diamond-blade paddle.

The shaft starts out as a 1¼-inch fir or spruce dowel or closet pole. The blade can be made from either 4 mm plywood or two layers of 3 mm plywood. Begin by cutting the dowel to the proper length. Use your saber saw to roughly shape the ends to the pattern shown on the plans. Use the sketches at the bottom of the plans to properly orient a feathered paddle's blades. With your spokeshave, carefully carve the scoop; measure the shape frequently so that you don't cut too far. Be careful to maintain the proper alignment between the two ends of the shaft. Use your block plane to shape the back of the shaft, then your spokeshave to narrow the throat and the hand grip. Work slowly and stop often to compare your work with the plans.

Lay out the blades to the shape shown on the plans and cut them out with your saber saw. Glue the blades to the shaft with thickened epoxy. Use several large clamps to hold the blade to the shaft. When the epoxy has cured, sand the paddle and coat it with a layer of unthickened epoxy.

FINISHING THE PADDLE

If you're hard on your paddles, you may want to apply a layer of thin (4-ounce) fiberglass cloth to the blades. This will greatly increase the paddle's durability. Stretch the cloth over the blade and brush on several coats of epoxy to saturate it. When the fiberglass has cured, sand the blade and apply another coat of epoxy to fill the pattern of the cloth. After the epoxy coating has cured, wash the paddle with soap and water to remove any amine blush. Sand the paddle again and finish it with several coats of marine varnish.

Paddling and Maintaining Your Kayak

Launch your new kayak in calm water; some kayaks, such as the West River 180, are high-performance boats that may seem quite tippy if you're not used to them. After a little practice this shouldn't be a problem, but it's best to get used to these boats on calm water. If this is your first kayak, please get a paddling and safety lesson. At the very least, you should know how to reenter a kayak in deep water by using a paddle float, and about the dangers of hypothermia. Always wear your personal flotation device, and take along a paddle float and a bilge pump. If your boat isn't fitted with bulkheads, it must be fitted with *flotation bags*; these plastic buoyancy bags fit into the bow and stern and are available at any kayak shop. If you're paddling in cold water, wear a wetsuit or, even better, a dry suit. It takes only a few minutes for hypothermia to set in if you wet-exit.

Ensure your kayak's long life by storing it under cover. If you don't have room at home, you might consider building a covered outdoor rack, renting a space at a local boathouse, or keeping the boat in a neighbor's garage. I store several kayaks by suspending them from the rafters in

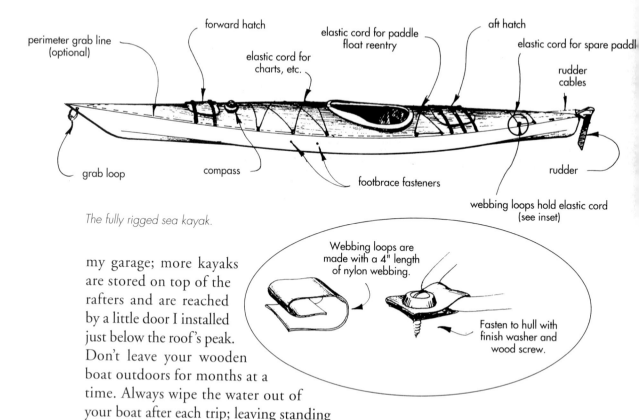

perimeter grab line (optional)

forward hatch

elastic cord for charts, etc.

elastic cord for paddle float reentry

aft hatch

elastic cord for spare paddle

rudder cables

grab loop

compass

footbrace fasteners

rudder

webbing loops hold elastic cord (see inset)

The fully rigged sea kayak.

Webbing loops are made with a 4" length of nylon webbing.

Fasten to hull with finish washer and wood screw.

my garage; more kayaks are stored on top of the rafters and are reached by a little door I installed just below the roof's peak. Don't leave your wooden boat outdoors for months at a time. Always wipe the water out of your boat after each trip; leaving standing water in a wooden boat is asking for rot. Remove all wet gear, and store your kayak with the hatches off.

Like all boats, your kayak will need a bit of maintenance to ensure its long life. Inevitably it will get scratched and banged up a little. If a scratch or ding penetrates into the wood, cover it with varnish as soon as the wood dries out. If the scratch is deep, level it out with epoxy first.

After a year or two of use, the varnish will start looking a little dull. This is the time to sand it lightly and brush on an additional coat. If you neglect it too long, it could start to crack and lift; then only a complete sanding—down to the epoxy—and new varnish will bring it back. Actually, taking a few hours each spring to lay on a fresh coat of varnish can be a strangely rewarding experience.

CHAPTER FOURTEEN

More Designs

The designs in this book won't meet every paddler's needs. If you build your own boat, you should get exactly what you want. So here are more of my designs in the hope that you'll find one that's just right for you. Think about how you'll use your new kayak and evaluate your paddling skills before picking a design to build. The plans for these boats are available from Chesapeake Light Craft (see the appendix for contact information).

Chesapeake 17, 18, LT16, LT17, and LT18

Since it is important that a kayak fit its paddler, I've drawn six versions of the popular Chesapeake kayak. The 17-footer has a beam of 24 inches and weighs 46 pounds. It's best for paddlers weighing between 160 and 220 pounds, with capacity for another 50 pounds of camping gear. If you're heavier, up to 270 pounds, you'll want to build the Chesapeake 18. This big boat, with a beam of 24½ inches and a weight of about 48 pounds, will carry a total burden of well over 300 pounds.

When I designed the Chesapeake kayaks, they were an instant hit among touring paddlers. But many paddlers who rarely camped from their kayaks asked for a lower-volume version for day paddling and the occasional weekend trip. So I went back to the computer and designed

ABOVE: *The Chesapeake 17 is a fine boat for rough-water touring or expeditions.* **LEFT:** *The Chesapeake double is simply a two-person version of the popular Chesapeake design.*

light-touring, or LT, versions of the Chesapeake. The Chesapeake LTs have the same proven hull shape as the original version but are lower and have a flatter aft deck. This reduces volume and windage and makes them a little lighter. Many shorter paddlers and Inuit-paddle devotees prefer the lower deck height and the resulting lower paddle position.

Chesapeake 21

The Chesapeake 21 is a large double or triple that is perfect for couples who need to carry a lot of gear in a fast, stable sea kayak. Its hull shape, based on that of the Chesapeake singles, exhibits the same

The North Bay is based on ancient West Greenland designs. It's fast, seaworthy, and demanding to paddle.

solid tracking, balance, and speed potential. In addition to the double shown in the bottom photo at left, there is a three-cockpit version that's ideal for families with a child who is not yet old enough to paddle. It's also a good choice for paddlers who simply must bring their St. Bernard along. (Don't laugh—I've received numerous calls from triple owners asking about doggy sprayskirts.) Before you decide to build a double or triple, remember that you'll always need someone to paddle it with you; these boats are simply too big to use as singles.

North Bay and North Bay XL

The North Bay is my interpretation of the classic West Greenland kayaks. Many paddlers feel that West Greenland kayaks rep-resented the highest form of kayak development. Indeed, it is difficult to argue with several thousand years of design evolution. I drew this design after studying numerous historical drawings of Inuit skin boats. But the North Bay is not based on any single boat; rather, it's based on the lines from several of the Inuit kayaks.

With a narrow hard-chine hull, the North Bay tracks like a train and is almost as fast. A flat aft deck and high ends make rolling a snap, which is significant. Rolls are very important given the North Bay's 20-inch beam. The boat's high-volume bow and stern and flared hull ensure great handling in rough water. This is not a roomy boat, and I would recommend it only for day paddling, and only for the expert paddler. Note that the standard cockpit is very small, in keeping with traditional design, though it could easily be enlarged.

The North Bay XL is a wider version of the same boat. It is virtually identical save for the 2 inches of extra beam and the larger cockpit. I designed this version for the many folks who could not comfortably fit into the original. The additional stability resulting from the extra beam makes this version suitable for athletic intermediate paddlers.

Patuxent 17.5 and 19.5

I designed the Patuxent 19.5 to be the fastest kit kayak available. It turned out to

The Patuxent 19.5 is probably the fastest kayak available in kit and plan form.

be one of the world's fastest sea kayaks, as proven by its continued success in races. Because of the boat's length, only a powerful paddler can take advantage of its speed potential. Less powerful and lighter paddlers may actually go faster (except during a sprint) in a shorter boat with a lower wetted-surface area. The Patuxent 19.5 is only 21 inches wide, so you should exercise caution in rough conditions; I capsized this boat while leading a local race, much to the amusement of my staff and fellow racers. The Patuxent 17.5 is a less extreme version for those of us who don't paddle flat-out most of the time. Both versions are of hard-chine construction with minimal fiberglass reinforcement and 3 mm decks to save weight. Obviously, neither version is as rugged as a touring boat. The Patuxent 19.5 is 19 feet, 6 inches long with a beam of 21 inches and a weight of 34 pounds. The 17.5 is 17 feet, 6 inches long with a 22-inch beam and a weight of 34 pounds.

Tred Avon

The Tred Avon is an older design for a medium-volume, coastal-touring double based on the old Cape Charles design. It has considerable rocker and is quite light for a double. I would say that the newer Chesapeake 21 is a better all-around double, but if you want a kayak with less volume and wetted-surface area, this would be a good choice. It can be built from only four 4-by-8 sheets of 4 mm plywood in either an open or a two-cockpit configuration. The LOA is 21 feet, the beam is 29 inches, and the weight is 55 pounds. I've also designed a triple version with a smaller center cockpit primarily for children.

West River 162 and 164

The West River 162 and 164 are strong, stable touring boats for paddlers who prefer a multi-chine hull shape. Their construction is almost identical to that of the West River 180. The 162 and 164 share the same basic hull shape, but the 164 has a higher freeboard and more room for gear and large feet. It is really very roomy for its length. Both models are 16 feet, 3 inches long, have a 24-inch beam, and weigh about 40 pounds.

Mill Creek 13, 15, and 16.5

I designed the Mill Creek kayaks as wider, shorter, and more stable alternatives to the typical sea kayak. They offer the stability sought by nature photographers, fly fishermen, and birders. Their large, open cockpits allow easy entry and exit, and the high coamings ensure a fairly dry cockpit even without a sprayskirt, which is important if you carry a camera or binoculars on your lap. I've also designed a sailing rig for all three Mill Creeks.

The Mill Creeks have simple, five-panel, multi-chine hulls with 6 mm bottoms and 4 mm sides and decks. Their waterlines are long, for good performance, and there is sufficient volume in the ends to handle rough conditions; in fact, I've paddled the 13-footer in 25-knot winds and 3-foot seas without difficulty.

The Mill Creek 13 has a 250-pound

The West River 164 is built like the West River 180, but it is shorter and more stable.

capacity and enough room for minimal camping gear. At just 13 feet long and 36 pounds, it's easy to carry down to the water and to cartop. This is my favorite kayak for fly-fishing; at least one professional fly-fishing guide on Florida Bay paddles this model. In fact, I would go so far as to say that of all the kayaks I've drawn, I am most proud of this one. It is not the fastest, nor the roomiest, nor even the prettiest, but once in a while everything in a boat design comes together just perfectly.

ABOVE: *The stable Mill Creek kayaks are ideal for fishing, photography, or birding.* **LEFT:** *The hard-chine Cape Charles and the compounded-plywood Pocomoke and Yare were the subjects of* The Kayak Shop.

The 15-foot version is longer, narrower, and carries more gear. This is the version for the touring paddler or anyone who seeks a little more performance in an open-cockpit kayak. The maximum load is 350 pounds.

The Mill Creek 16.5 is a very versatile boat. In addition to being a wonderful open-cockpit double, it is small enough to be used as a single once in a while. And if you get tired of paddling, drop in a sliding-seat rowing unit; it rows better than a few purpose-built rowing craft I've tried. If you feel lazy, step the mast and leeboard and let the wind do all the work. Several builders have even installed electric outboard motors. The Mill Creek 16.5 is a little small for long-distance touring for two, but if you pack light . . .

Older Kayak Designs

Several of my kayak designs, including the three shown in *The Kayak Shop*, have been replaced by newer designs.

The first of these is the Cape Charles 18, featured in *The Kayak Shop*. There is also a Cape Charles 17, 15.5, and 13.5. Thousands of these kayaks have been built all over the world and most seem to still be in use. I've received literally hundreds of letters from their owners praising the design. Still, I feel that the new Chesapeake is in every way a superior boat. It is faster, easier to build, stronger, better balanced, more seaworthy, and tracks better.

The low-volume, compounded-plywood Yare, also featured in *The Kayak Shop*, is much like the Severn but longer and narrower. I've also received many letters praising this design, but as a practical touring boat it is simply too small and too tender. Most of the Yare's many fans are lighter paddlers who want a fast and light boat with minimal wetted-surface area. Today, I would build a Patuxent or West River instead.

The Pocomoke, the third design in *The Kayak Shop*, is also a compounded-plywood kayak, but unlike the Severn and the Yare, it has a keelson to which the hull panels are nailed. The Pocomoke is a small double best suited to day paddling. It is also the most difficult to build of the boats I've designed, plus it is designed to be built from 5- by 10-foot sheets of 4 mm plywood, which have become very difficult to find.

Canoes, Pulling Boats, and Sailboats

Most paddlers enjoy messing around in all sorts of boats, not just kayaks, and I am no exception; over the years I've become an avid oarsman and a sailor as well as a paddler. So it's only natural that I've drawn designs for a number of other types of craft. If you share my love for all sorts of boats, you may find these interesting.

For many years I resisted designing canoes. Most canoes were too big and heavy, and the shapes didn't lend themselves to plywood construction. But imagine an elegant lapstrake canoe so light that you can put it on your shoulder and stroll casually down a trail to a hidden lake. That was the idea behind the classic *trapper*, or *pack*, canoes. The Sassafras 12 is my interpretation of those craft. It is 12 feet long, weighs only 26 pounds, can carry 225 pounds, and is propelled by a double paddle. I was so pleased with the 12-footer that I drew 14- and 16-foot versions meant to be used with single-blade paddles. All three are built using the Lap-Stitch method of stitch-and-glue construction. This is similar to multi-chine construction, but the panels overlap using a special rabbet joint to give the appearance of a traditional lapstrake hull.

Perhaps I shouldn't admit this in a book about kayaks, but in recent years I've spent more time in rowing shells than in kayaks. The reason is that the hour or so each day that I can devote to exercise is more effectively spent rowing. Kayaking may be the best way to enjoy scenery, but

TOP: *Even canoes can be built using the stitch-and-glue method. This Sassafras 16 was designed to showcase a new type of stitch-and-glue construction called LapStitch.* **MIDDLE:** *Though kayaking is the best way to explore, a rowing shell such as this Oxford Shell provides wonderful exercise.* **BOTTOM:** *The Annapolis Wherry is my favorite rowing boat. It is fast, stable, seaworthy, and beautiful.*

ABOVE: *There's nothing like taking a friend sailing, especially in a boat as nice as this Jimmy Skiff.*
RIGHT: *The bolt-on SailRig turns any kayak into a fast trimaran.*

if you want a quick aerobic workout, nothing beats a sliding-seat rowing boat.

My favorite shell is the Annapolis Wherry, a 17-foot, 9-inch, fast rowing boat built using the LapStitch method. Though the Annapolis Wherry can be rowed in normal fixed-seat fashion, it is at its best when powered by a sliding-seat rig. I've also designed a higher-performance rowing shell, the Oxford Shell, but on the often choppy water near our house I prefer the stability of the wherry.

It has often been said that good skiffs are among the easiest boats to build yet the hardest to design. I think that the Jimmy Skiff, my adaptation of the classic Chesapeake Bay crabbing skiff, is a "good skiff." It makes a fine sailing and rowing craft. At 13 feet and 95 pounds, it is small and light enough to cartop, yet it will carry a family of four. The Jimmy Skiff's simple sprit sailing rig can be set up in about 5 minutes; I can think of no better boat in which to learn how to sail. Of course, you might prefer to leave the sailing rig off, ship some oars, and go fishing or crabbing, as generations of watermen here on the Chesapeake Bay have done.

And, finally, you can turn your kayak into a sailboat with the outrigger sailing system I designed. This rig, shown in the bottom photo on page 183, allows a kayak to sail as well as a small daysailer and can be easily dismantled for cartopping.

There you have it—a lot of boats to choose from and an easy way to build them. Get to work, and I'll see you on the water!

Further Reading

BOOKS ABOUT KAYAK BUILDING

Dyson, George. *Baidarka*. Edmonds WA: Alaska Northwest, 1986. Building kayaks based on native designs from aluminum tubing and nylon.

Ellis, George. *Paddlemaking 101*. Self-published, 1998. Available from Chesapeake Light Craft. Making a traditional Inuit paddle.

Gougeon Brothers. *The Gougeon Brothers on Boat Construction: Wood & WEST SYSTEM Materials*. New rev. (4th) ed. Bay City MI: Gougeon Brothers, 1985. The bible of wood-epoxy construction.

Putz, George. *Wood and Canvas Kayak Building*. Camden ME: International Marine, 1990. Canvas on frame kayaks.

Wittman, Rebecca J. *Brightwork: The Art of Finishing Wood*. Camden ME: International Marine, 1990. Looking for the ultimate finish.

PERIODICALS

Atlantic Coastal Kayaker
29 Burley St.
Wenham MA 01984
Primarily about sea kayaking on the East Coast, but it occasionally contains articles on boatbuilding.

Boatbuilder
P.O. Box 3000
Denville NJ 07834
Largely about building large boats, but many of the techniques can be used in building kayaks, and *Boatbuilder* does occasionally run a piece on kayaks.

Fine Woodworking
Taunton Press
P.O. Box 5506
Newtown CT 06470
Though devoted largely to furniture making and tool reviews, this magazine is well written and will interest any woodworker.

Messing about in Boats
29 Burley St.
Wenham MA 01984
This iconoclastic little biweekly devotes much space to home-built boats, weird designs, and getting out on the water on the cheap. It's fun and inexpensive, and I urge you to subscribe.

Notes From Our Shop
1805 George Ave.
Annapolis MD 21401
This free newsletter from Chesapeake Light Craft contains articles and shop tips related to kayak building.

Sea Kayaker
6327 Seaview Ave. NW
Seattle WA 98107
The editor of this magazine for hard-core sea kayakers is a kayak builder who regularly publishes articles on kayak building.

WoodenBoat
P.O. Box 78
Brooklin ME 04616
Thick, glossy, and chock-full of well-written articles, *WoodenBoat* is simply the best magazine on the subject of boatbuilding.

Suppliers

Listed below are companies I've done business with and that I can recommend, as well as companies that have been recommended to me by friends or other boatbuilders. Other suppliers can be found by looking through the ads in *WoodenBoat*. Companies that sell paddles, sprayskirts, and other gear often advertise in *Sea Kayaker*.

Boulter Plywood Corp.
24 Broadway
Somerville MA 02145

Chesapeake Light Craft
1805 George Ave.
Annapolis MD 21401
410-267-0137
www.clcboats.com
Plans and kits for the boats in this book, plywood, epoxy, hardware, and accessories.

Chesapeake Marine Fasteners
10 Willow St.
Annapolis MD 21401

Clark Craft
16 Aqua Ln.
Tonawanda NY 14150
Kayak plans.

M. L. Condon Co.
260 Ferris Ave.
White Plains NY 10603
Lumber and plywood.

Eden Saw
211 Seton Rd.
Port Townsend WA 98368
www.edensaw.com
Lumber and plywood.

Flounder Bay Boat Lumber
1019 3rd St.
Anacortes WA 98221
Plywood.

Harbor Sales Co.
1000 Harbor Ct.
Sudlersville MD 21668
Plywood.

Jamestown Distributors
28 Narragansett Ave.
Jamestown RI 02835
Epoxy, hardware, fiberglass tape, and a wide range of boatbuilding supplies and tools.

Garrett Wade
161 Ave. of the Americas
New York NY 10013
Tools.

WoodenBoat Store
P.O. Box 78
Brooklin ME 04616
Kayak plans.

METRIC CONVERSION TABLE

1 inch	2.54 centimeters
1 inch	25.4 millimeters
1 foot	0.3 meters
1 yard	0.914 meters
1 pound	0.45 kilograms
1 ounce	28.35 grams
1 gallon	3.785 kilograms
1 knot	1.85 kilometers/hour
1 mile/hour	1.609 kilometers/hour
1 nautical mile	1.85 kilometers
°F	°C × 1.8 + 32
°C	(°F − 32) × 0.555

INDEX

Page numbers in **bold** refer to pages with illustrations